D0624929

GANDHI

A PICTORIAL BIOGRAPHY

ART CENTER COLLEGE OF DESIGN LIBRARY
1700 LIDA STREET
PASADENA, CALIFORNIA 91103

954.0350924
G 195
G 618

GANDHI

A PICTORIAL BIOGRAPHY

Text by Gerald Gold

Photograph Selection and Afterword by

Richard Attenborough

Newmarket Press

New York

ART CENTER COLLEGE OF DESIGN LIBRARY
1700 LIDA STREET
PASADENA, CALIFORNIA 91103

Text and design © 1983 Newmarket Press

Historical photographs courtesy of the National Gandhi Museum,
New Delhi, India. All other photographs from the film *Gandhi*
© 1982 Indo-British Films Ltd. Frank Connor, photographer.

All rights reserved.

The publisher wishes to acknowledge the support and cooperation
of Columbia Pictures in the publication of this book.

The publisher also appreciates the help of Dr. Razi Ahmad,
Director, and Ramsharan Sharma of the National Gandhi Museum.

This book may not be reproduced in whole or in part,
in any form, without permission. Inquiries should be
addressed to Newmarket Press, 3 East 48th Street,
New York, New York 10017

FIRST EDITION 1 2 3 4 5 6 7 8 9 0

Library of Congress Cataloging in Publication Data

Gold, Gerald.
  Gandhi, a pictorial biography.

  Bibliography: p.
  Includes index.
  1. Gandhi, Mahatma, 1869–1948.   2. Statesman—India—
Biography.   I. Title.
DS481.G3G584   1983   954.03'5'0924 [B]   82-22478
ISBN 0-937858-27-7
ISBN 0-937858-20-X (pbk.)

Manufactured in the United States of America

Design by H. Roberts Design

Contents

Introduction

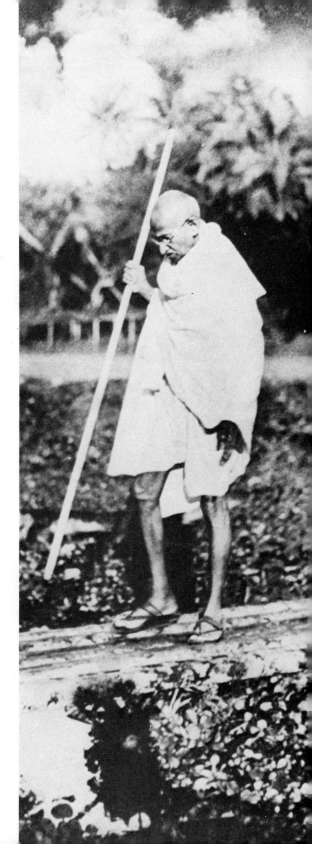

IMAGES. Images of the man and his people. Images of Gandhi and India. The story of Gandhi is filled to bursting with images. Of the callow bridegroom overcome by the guilt of his lust, of the shy Indian law student in London wandering the streets looking for a vegetarian restaurant, of the young, Europe-oriented barrister rallying the rich and poor Indians of South Africa to fight for their rights as human beings.

Images of the holy man in white loincloth traveling the vastness of India preaching his message of truth, nonviolence, and noncooperation. Of fighting the British with strikes and marches and prayers—and with the ever present example of his own ascetic life, an example of poverty and goodness and love that endeared him to India's millions, bewildered and frustrated the British, and brought him adulation and imitation around the world.

Images of the man squatting in a jail cell at a spinning wheel, writing and talking and spinning. Images of the man scooping a handful of salt from the sea and thereby sounding the death knell of empire. Images of the man, wan and emaciated, fasting for an end to the abomination of untouchability, or for an end to Hindu-Moslem fratricide. Images of the man joking with children, or sitting at a conference table with officials, chiding and cajoling and sometimes overcoming his opposition by sheer will.

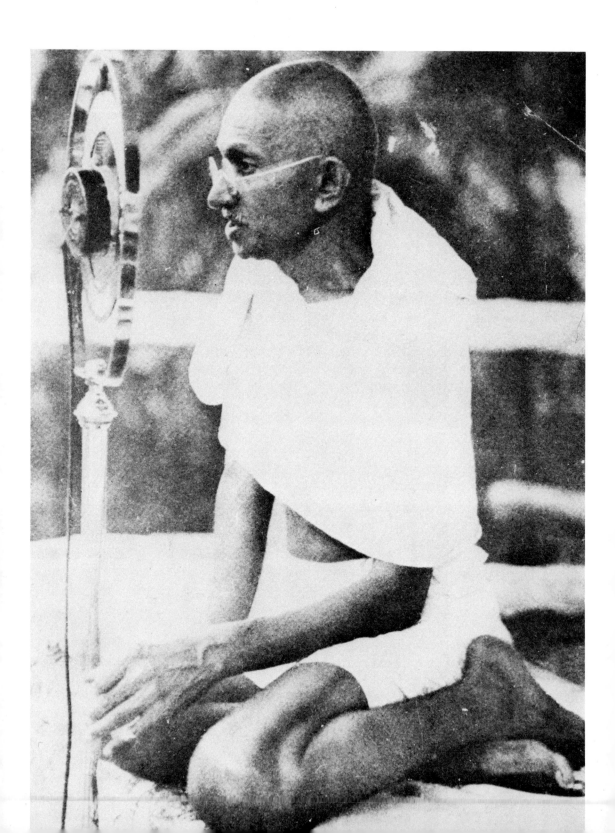

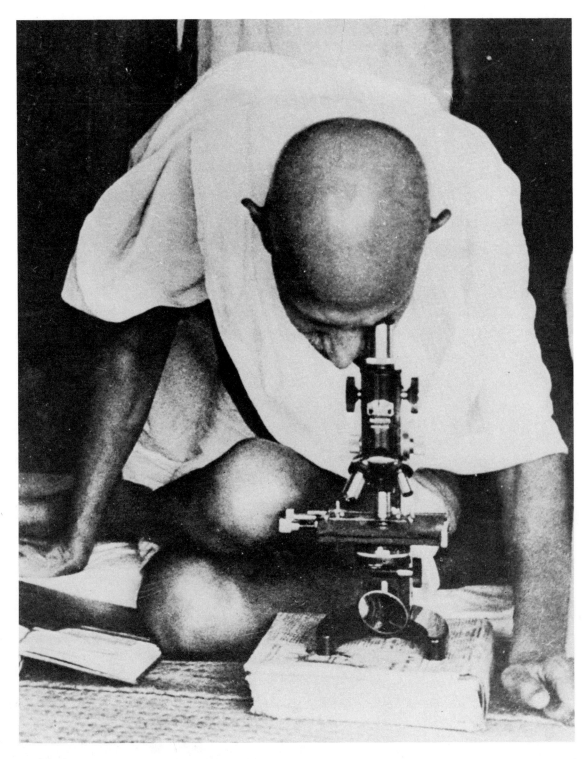

Gandhi brought a sense of nationwide purpose to India under British rule, and a sense of India's religious heritage to his countrymen in a way no one had before and no one has since.

His story is one of courage and determination and religious will. It is a story that in many ways is strange to the West, for the combination of religious fervor and political acumen is not one ordinarily seen in the West. But for India it was natural. It needed only the right man. Even those who disagreed with him admired and respected him, and to his followers he was a saint.

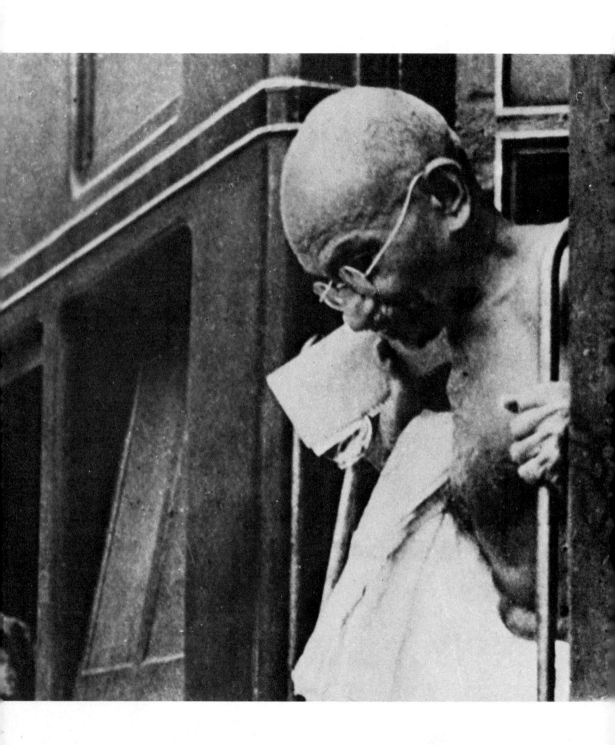

Images. Images, too, because he knew how to use the world of images—the newspaper, the camera—to foster his ideas and ideals. He wrote ceaselessly—books, pamphlets, thousands of newspaper articles for his own papers, as well as thousands of letters. He was always accessible to the press, and his greatest campaigns for independence were carefully planned for maximum dramatic impact on his people and on world opinion.

Beginnings

Mohandas Karamchand Gandhi was born in Porbandar, India, a western coastal city on the Kathiawar Peninsula, on October 2, 1869. His family was of the banyan caste—technically businessmen or merchants—and the name Gandhi means "grocer." His father, Karamchand Gandhi, was neither a businessman nor a grocer, but a relatively well-to-do official of the state of Porbandar, whose office had been handed down in the family. Porbandar was one of the countless tiny princely states that the British had decided not to bother (except for taxes) and in some cases had even created as insurance against a general uprising in India. Gandhi's mother, Putliba, was Karamchand's fourth wife, two having died and one perhaps unable to bear children, and Mohandas was the fourth and last child of the couple. There were two brothers—Laxmidas, the eldest son, and Karsandas, and a sister, Raliatbehn, the oldest of the four, who outlived all of them and died when she was almost a hundred years old.

Gandhi's father was hot-tempered but had a reputation for sturdy integrity. This integrity several times got him into trouble with his rulers, but it also got him out of trouble because it was recognized as an overriding quality. Gandhi's father had had a little schooling, but his mother had none, and she could neither read nor write. She was extremely devout, however, minutely observing religious vows for self-purification and self-discipline, and was given to frequent and extended fasting. It is clear where Gandhi got some of the impulses that were later to become cornerstones of his religious outlook, of his morality, and of his political methods.

Gandhi writes:

"The outstanding impression my mother has left on my memory is that of saintliness. She was deeply religious. She would not think of taking her meals without her daily prayers. She would take the hardest vows and keep them without flinching. To keep two or three consecutive fasts was nothing to her."

Once in the rainy season she vowed not to have food without seeing the sun. Her children would watch, and as the sun broke through the clouds they would run to tell her. "She would run out to see with her own eyes," Gandhi recalled, "but by that time the fugitive sun would be gone, thus depriving her of her meal. 'That does not matter,' she would say cheerfully. 'God did not want me to eat today.' And then she would return to her round of duties."

This asceticism, while very much in the Hindu tradition, was rather out of the ordinary, and there is no doubt that it had a profound effect on young Mohandas. From his earliest school

Karamchand Gandhi, father of Mohandas

20   Gandhi's mother, Putliba.

BIRTH PLACE OF MAHATMA GANDHIJI. A.D. 2.10. 1869.

The house in Porbandar where Gandhi was born in 1869.

days these ascetic qualities were in the forefront of Gandhi's thinking. They served later first to create a saintly aura about him that was an important factor in his popularity in a country whose greatest heroes were religious men. Besides that, his frugal way of living provided an unassailable backdrop to his highly controversial political acts; it was impossible to attack the man in personal terms.

In his childhood Gandhi attended a temple where readings were taken alternately from the Hindu Bhagavad Gita and from the Moslem Koran, and Porbandar itself was a seaport that looked out to the world and therefore harbored some two dozen religions. Gandhi from his earliest years developed a tolerant attitude toward all religions—which, in a convoluted way, came back to haunt him at the end of his life.

Gandhi's childhood was not so different from that of other boys, except that he had an unusually developed sense of responsibility and duty. He did what other boys did, including things he wasn't supposed to do, but he often felt terribly guilty about his escapades, and would draw morals from his actions and reactions even as a youngster. He and a friend would pick up an uncle's cigarette butts and smoke them, and even got to the point of stealing servants' pocket money to buy cigarettes. They guiltily and boyishly contemplated suicide, but Gandhi finally just gave it all up as a silly business. He left the experiment behind and ever after inveighed against smoking as unhealthy.

Mohandas Gandhi at age seven.

As for school, Gandhi had no illusions. "It was with some difficulty that I got through the multiplication tables. The fact that I recollect nothing more of those days than having learnt, in company with other boys, to call our teacher all kinds of names, would strongly suggest that my intellect must have been sluggish, and my memory raw."

When Gandhi was about seven years old, his father got a new post, as *dewan* or prime minister in Rajkot, about five days' journey from Porbandar by cart. Schooling continued, and life was pretty much the same until 1882, when Gandhi's life changed drastically and irrevocably. He was thirteen years old and he was married to a girl the same age who had been chosen for him. Kasturba Makanji was the daughter of a Porbandar merchant. She had had no schooling, but, like Gandhi, lived in comfortable circumstances.

Because of the often ruinous expense involved in an elaborate Hindu wedding, Gandhi was married simultaneously with his brother Karsandas (Laxmidas was already married) and a cousin. Neither Gandhi nor his bride nor the parents nor anyone else found anything out of the ordinary in the marriage. Child marriage was commonly accepted, as was having one's mate chosen by the parents. In later years Gandhi was to attack the custom with great bitterness, but for now the highly sexed young man was not concerned with such issues.

At the ceremony at Kasturba's home in Porbandar they followed the Hindu custom of walking seven steps around a fire, reciting the marriage vows.

"Take one step, that we may have strength of will," the bridegroom said.

"In every worthy wish of yours, I shall be your helpmate," the bride replied.

"Take the second step, that we may be filled with vigor," said Gandhi.

"In every worthy wish of yours, I shall be your helpmate," Kasturba responded.

"Take the third step, that we may live in ever-increasing prosperity."

"Your joys and sorrows I will share."

"Take the fourth step, that we may be ever full of joy."

"I will ever live devoted to you, speaking words of love and praying for your happiness."

"Take the fifth step, that we may serve the people."

"I will follow close behind you always and help you to keep your vow of serving the people."

"Take the sixth step, that we may follow our religious vows in life."

"I will follow you in observing our religious vows and duties."

"Take the seventh step, that we may ever live as friends."

"It is the fruit of my good deeds that I have you as my husband. You are my best friend, my highest guru, and my sovereign lord."

The words were traditional, and for such youngsters probably without solemn meaning. But some of the vows—especially those about living as "friends" and "serving the people" were to take on extraordinary significance for the couple in the more than sixty years of their marriage.

Like most Indian child brides and bridegrooms, the couple lived more apart than together over the next few years, each spending some time together and then living separately in their parents' homes.

Gandhi reported with chagrin later that he was a stupidly jealous husband, without any cause whatever, and comments that "I must say I was passionately fond of her. Even at school I used to think of her, and the thought of nightfall and our subsequent meeting was ever haunting me. I have already said that Kasturba was illiterate. I was very anxious to teach her, but lustful love left me no time."

Aside from schooling and marriage, one other great problem seems to have confronted Gandhi in these years—meat eating. Hindus, of course, are traditionally vegetarians, but during Gandhi's early years meat eating was considered by some as daring and progressive and a way to counter the might of the British raj—meat eating, it was thought, would make one stronger and better able to fight the colonial power. Gandhi went on at length about his meat-eating experiments with a radical school friend, a Moslem, and describes how his friends would tempt him with all sorts of delicacies. Not long after, however, Gandhi gave up meat—not because he felt it was wrong, at that time, so much as because he could not bear to go on lying to his parents. He never told them, and in later years he

regarded meat—and almost every other food—with suspicion.

This passion for truth telling was to become a cornerstone of his philosophy and basis for his civil disobedience campaigns. But it also resulted in some of the most extraordinarily frank autobiographical confessions ever put on paper—and by a man whom many came to regard as a saint.

Gandhi told how, in 1885, his father was dying, and how he would sit with him and nurse him for hours on end, rejoicing in the opportunity to serve. Kasturba was pregnant at the time. Gandhi relates:

"The dreadful night came. It was 10:30 or 11:00 p.m. I was giving massage. My uncle offered to relieve me. I was glad and went straight to the bedroom. My wife, poor thing, was fast asleep. I woke her. In five or six minutes, however, the servant knocked at the door." The news was that Karamchand had died.

Gandhi continued:

"I saw that, if animal passion had not blinded me, I should have been spared the torture of separation from my father during his last moments. It is a blot I have never been able to efface or forget, and I have always thought that, although my devotion to my parents knew no bounds and I would have given up anything for it, yet it was weighed and found unpardonably wanting because my mind was at the same moment in the grip of lust."

Gandhi was almost as upset about the fact of having had this "carnal

Gandhi at age 14 (right) with a classmate

desire" with a pregnant wife and saw proper retribution for this sin in the fact that "the poor mite that was born to my wife" lived only three or four days.

A few years later, in 1888, the Gandhis' first child to live was born. It was a son, named Harilal, the first of four children, all boys.

Gandhi in 1886, when he was 17.

Certain threads run through all the writings by and about Gandhi, including obsessions with truth, diet, and sex. All were central to his thought, and all had profound effects on his way of seeing the world. If there was one thing that tied them all together in a practical way it was the urge to experiment—with telling the truth under all circumstances, even when the truth resulted in short-term damage; with constantly worrying over the kinds of food one should eat, and how they affected the psyche and the body; with seeking chastity or "pure love." This bent for experiment had cropped up already in Gandhi's boyish cigarette smoking, meat eating, and in telling the truth in school even though it may have meant punishment.

His biggest experiment as a youth was about to take place. He determined to study law in England— he was the first in his family to go to England—despite the opposition of his family, and especially his mother, who feared that her son's religious purity would be hopelessly undermined by wine and women in England. He was adamant, however, and despite his generally lackluster showing in school—although he had managed to attend a small college near Rajkot— and despite his being in effect excommunicated by his caste, he sailed for England on September 4, 1888, to a life that, in a strange way, reinforced the standards his mother had given him.

England

Mohandas K. Gandhi when he was a law student in London.

England proved a trial to Gandhi. He felt out of place, bewildered, strange. Although ultimately he made many friends and became active in several organizations, this initial strangeness turned him in on himself and his Indian heritage and led him to the fringes rather than the mainstream of English life. Whereas future colleagues like Jawaharlal Nehru took away from their years in England a lifelong pattern of upper-class English habits and standards, Gandhi's personality became more Indian, more Hindu.

His ascetic bent and his vegetarian

Gandhi, bottom row right, with members of the London Vegetarian Society in 1890.

vows gave him problems as soon as he got to England—not to mention the white flannel suit he was wearing when he disembarked in Southampton. Somewhere he had picked up the idea that all Englishmen wore white suits, but of course everyone he saw was wearing a dark suit. He was mortally embarrassed. Even worse, he found it impossible to get a square meal without meat, and for days he wandered about London or hid in his room, hungry all the time. (Despite his later reputation for fasting and asceticism he always had a hearty appetite, and forgoing food was difficult for him.) One friend kept imploring him to eat meat, but Gandhi was adamant. Almost comically ignorant, he did not know there were vegetarian restaurants. When he heard there were, he would wander about London ten or twelve hours a day in search of one, but without success, and ended up going into cheap restaurants and gorging on bread, which never satisfied him. One day he found a vegetarian restaurant in Farringdon Street. More than a quarter of a century later he recalled:

"The sight of it filled me with the same joy a child feels at getting a thing after his own heart. Before I entered I noticed books for sale exhibited under a glass window near the door. I saw among them Salt's *Plea for Vegetarianism*. This I purchased for a shilling and went straight to the dining room. It was my first hearty meal since my arrival in England. God had come to my aid."

Henry Salt introduced him to the first structured reasoning he had ever heard about vegetarianism and provided the initial impetus for Gandhi's lifelong experiments with diet—a subject on which he thereafter felt himself an authority.

But vegetarianism gave him more: it was his route to involvement with the eccentric, experimental, modern English mind, and its influence on him was profound. The vegetarian movement was more than a food faddist cult. Its members were in many respects in the vanguard of social thought in England. They were connected with or had sympathies with many of the other currents then roiling British intellectual life on such subjects as Victorian marriage, sex, contraception, religion, and socialism. While many vegetarians were merely food faddists, many were much more, and Gandhi's connections with them gave him a window on all these elements, although almost all of them, it is true, could be classified at the time as eccentric.

One of the most notable figures in this fringe area was the Russian-born Madame Blavatsky, who had come to England and in 1875 founded the Theosophical Society, which had strong ties to Hinduism, Buddhism, and vegetarianism, as well as elements of the occult and the mystical. Madame Blavatsky and her disciple, Annie Besant, preached that Theosophy was an eternal religion containing within it all others, that "there is no religion higher than the truth," a concept that found fertile ground in Gandhi's mind.

**A portrait of
Gandhi when he was
studying law.**

Gandhi met the leaders of many of these organizations, including Henry Salt and Annie Besant, and before long he was involved with vegetarian groups and their newsletters, writing occasional articles, and even speaking at meetings.

He also was introduced to orthodox Christian thought and got a taste of the Bible; even more importantly he got for the first time a look at his Indianism and Hinduism through western eyes, partly by reading Sir Edwin Arnold's English translation of the Bhagavad Gita, which, along with the Ramayana, is one of the two great Indian epics and a cornerstone of Hinduism.

Two of the principal concepts from the Gita have been fixtures in Hindu thought for thousands of years, and have been constantly revived in western thought as well, even up to today. One is *karma*, fate or destiny. The idea of *karma* has been used for centuries to justify caste in India, and with it the existence of noncaste people, or Untouchables, who were to be a focus of much of Gandhi's thought and action over the years. The other concept is that of *darma*—the other side of the coin—man's free will and his obligation to do the best he can with his *karma*. Untouchables were thought to have been put at the bottom of the human heap because of their failure to live properly during a previous life. By submitting to his station in life, but by doing his mean tasks as faithfully as possible and living a pure life, an Untouchable could expect to return in yet another life in a higher caste.

Other directions that Gandhi was to follow also became evident in his London years. At one point, as if to try to overcome his feelings of inadequacy as he moved in English society, he became rather a dandy, buying expensive, stylishly cut clothes and spending endless time on his appearance. Out of this, though, grew a realization that he was being foolish: dressing English wouldn't make him English, and he abruptly stopped his spendthrift way with clothes. Typically, however, he continued to wear the clothes to get his money's worth out of them.

He also realized he was paying rent for a room with meals, but wasn't eating the meals since the homes he lived in were not vegetarian homes. He therefore decided to move to a place where he did his own cooking and—with a sharp sense of guilt over the fact that his brother back in India was footing the bill for his lavish ways—started keeping minutely detailed accounts of every penny he spent, a practice that was to become a byword for every spiritual community or political organization with which he was involved in later years.

Gandhi also sharpened his English (his native language was Gujarati), got a smattering of other languages, started to read newspapers, and acquired a respect and admiration for British fairness that was never to leave him, although at times it was the memory rather than the reality that he was thinking of.

London also meant years of reading books—reading strictly for information and understanding, never for pleasure alone. He read widely about religion and ethics and history and of course law, and on June 10, 1891, after passing his examinations, he was called to the bar. He was enrolled in the High Court on June 11, and on June 12 he sailed for India and home, and for the child bride who was no longer a child.

Gandhi was still the shy boy who had left India full of self-doubt but full of determination. "Notwithstanding my study," he wrote, "there was no end to my helplessness and fear. I did not feel myself qualified to practice law." An uncertain future stretched out before him.

Gandhi was right to be fearful. India seemed to have little to offer him. He tried several law jobs obtained through family and London contacts, but could not make a go of them. Once he showed up in court but found himself unable to utter a word. Even with his brother's connections (Laxmidas was an attorney and was doing fairly well), nothing seemed to go right for him. His return had been dampened considerably from the start when he learned that his mother had died while he was in London; his family had kept it from him, so as not to interfere with his studies. Furthermore, he was now the father of a second son, Manilal, who was born less than a year after he returned. Gandhi thought about following his father's footsteps into state politics, but his family's influence had waned, and even Laxmidas was having problems.

Thus it was with no little relief that Gandhi accepted a job that had been offered to him through Laxmidas, to serve as an attorney in South Africa for an Indian Moslem trading firm that had many business interests there. Less than two years after returning home, Gandhi set out in April 1893 to work for Dada Abdullah and Company. Again he left Kasturba and his family behind.

So far he had been, if not a total failure in India and England, then hardly a smashing success. No one recognized in him, and he did not recognize in himself, any call to greatness. South Africa was to change all that.

Gandhi in South Africa.

South Africa

South Africa was the laboratory for India. Gandhi accomplished great feats in South Africa, but none of it lasted very long after he left. As one biographer put it, "what Gandhi did to South Africa was, however, less important than what South Africa did to him."

It focused and sharpened his thinking, set him unwaveringly on the course of truth, nonviolence, and civil disobedience, taught him how to organize, how to oppose, how to move masses of people to do his bidding, how to make his religious convictions and moral principles essential parts of his politics. His reading of the Gita and the Bible had left him with the indelible conviction that man must fight evil always and that the way to fight was to turn the other cheek—to fight back only with love and truth and a fierce unwillingness to submit to injustice and cruelty. In South Africa, through his experience and his reading—especially of Tolstoy and Ruskin—he came to powerful conclusions about the worthiness of man's labor and about the need for peaceful opposition to discrimination and racism. When he left South Africa at the end of twenty years, all his main ideas had been formed and tested in action.

There is no neat explanation for the transformation of Gandhi from shy and

Gandhi in Johannesburg, South Africa in 1907.

less-than-competent barrister to fiery leader of men within a week of his arriving in South Africa. Perhaps it was simply that he felt less self-conscious about his shortcomings among Indians in the far outpost of the British empire than he did in an India burdened with centuries of tradition and surrounded by high-powered lawyers and others whose brilliance left him tongue-tied. In South Africa, among Indians, at

least, he was the highly educated one, the barrister, the man with an English education in law.

The South Africa to which Gandhi came had some 65,000 Indians at the time, compared to half a million whites and 2 million blacks. His

C. F. (Charlie) Andrews (left) and W. W. Pearson standing behind Gandhi.

Indian compatriots were of two kinds—Moslem businessmen (many of them wealthy) and their Hindu and Parsi clerks on one hand, and indentured laborers (really slaves) on the other hand. The latter, the vast majority, were looked down on not only by the whites but by the Indian white-collar workers. Democratically, the whites contemptuously called all Indians "Sammy," from the common Indian word *swami*.

The Indian businessmen accepted the social injustices they faced every day and spent their energy on making money. Gandhi, though, had come away from England with a strong sense of justice and of British fair play; even in India he had attributed British injustices to individuals rather than to the system or to Englishmen as a group. In later years he was to operate on exactly the opposite principle.

Affronts to his sense of law and fair play seemed to touch off an explosion that almost automatically led to action. Within weeks he was the leader of the Indian community in Britain's Natal territory of South Africa, where more than 50,000 of South Africa's Indians lived.

When Gandhi landed in Durban, Natal, he was met by his employer Dada Abdullah, and quickly got his first taste of the disdain with which Indians were treated. A judge ordered him to remove the Bengali turban he wore, even though he was otherwise attired in western style. He refused, with Abdullah's persuasion (although he first thought of acceding) and immediately wrote to a local

andhi while he was in South Africa.

ART CENTER COLLEGE OF DESIGN LIBRARY
1700 LIDA STREET

Kasturba with the Gandhi sons, around 1903.
Left, Gandhi (center) with office colleagues
in Johannesburg, South Africa.

newspaper, gaining his first small notoriety, as the letter provoked controversy.

A week later Abdullah sent him to Pretoria, in the Boer-ruled Transvaal, for the business for which he had been hired, and it was on that rail journey that Gandhi got his next important lesson—one that was to set in motion all his powers. Abdullah had obtained a first-class ticket for him, and Gandhi blithely boarded the train. When the train reached Pietermaritzburg, Gandhi was quietly reading. A European passenger passed his compartment, saw the brown-skinned Gandhi, and summoned a railroad employee to put the coolie, or kaffir, out of the first-class coach. Gandhi explained that he had a first-class ticket, but to no avail. Indians simply didn't ride in first class. He refused to move to the third-class coach and was forcibly put off the train, along with his luggage. He spent the cold night shivering in the station, refusing to get his coat from his luggage, because he would not deal with the stationmaster.

The indignity and shock of the affair were a revelation. In India he had little to do with Europeans, and in London he had been welcomed into the homes of Englishmen, many of whom became close friends. On that very night the idea of action took root. "The hardship to which I was subjected was superficial—only a symptom of the deep disease of color prejudice. I should try, if possible, to root out the disease and suffer hardships in the process. Redress for the wrongs I should seek only to the extent that

would be necessary for the removal of the color prejudice."

The next morning he sent a telegram to the railroad management, which helped to get him proper passage to Pretoria. His Indian friends told him his experience was not unusual, but Gandhi could not accept the situation, and within a few days of reaching Pretoria he invited Indians there to a series of meetings at which he suggested forming an organization. He made sure the British agent in the city learned of the Indians' grievances, although the Transvaal was a Boer state and outside British jurisdiction.

Gandhi also began to learn about the discriminatory laws in the Transvaal. Indians could not own property, except in specific areas, could not vote, and had to pay an annual tax of three pounds. Indians had to be off the streets by 9:00 p.m. or, if they were working for Europeans, had to have a pass permitting them to be outdoors after curfew.

For the next year Gandhi threw himself into the court case he had been hired to work on—a case involving a dispute between Indian merchants—and started another round of reading, almost entirely books on religion, with the help of a European Christian who kept trying to convert him. Among the books he read was Tolstoy's *The Kingdom of God Is Within You*, which renounced the use of force and preached "inward perfection, truth, and love" and which reinforced conclusions Gandhi was already coming to about how to deal with the forces of injustice. Tolstoy's

From left, Gandhi, his secretary Sonja Schlesin, and Herman Kallenbach in Johannesburg.

vision fit in with the Hindu idea of *ahimsa*—nonviolence in all thought and action—but went beyond *ahimsa,* which was merely a negative way of avoiding violence. Tolstoy saw in nonviolence an active method of conduct.

By April 1894 the lawsuit had ended (Gandhi had successfully promoted a compromise settlement) and the young lawyer prepared to leave South Africa, his job over. On the day of departure, Dada Abdullah organized a going-away party. Quite by accident, Gandhi picked up a newspaper and saw an item about proposed legislation that would take the vote away from the Indians in Natal. Most Indians did not bother to vote anyway, and so were not especially upset, but Gandhi could not let the situation go unchallenged, seeing in the legislation the beginning of what could be a mortal blow to Indian self-respect.

Before anyone realized what was happening, the people at the going-away party became a committee to fight the legislation, and Gandhi's friends and employers were begging him to stay on and organize to fight. He agreed but refused payment, saying that he could not accept money for public service. Instead, he asked a number of the merchants to retain him as their attorney, which assured him a steady income. He then rapidly set about sending telegrams to the Natal Assembly, circulated petitions, and wrote to the press. By August he had decided that a committee was not enough—all Indians in Natal needed a wider forum.

Taking his cue from India, he organized the Indian Natal Congress, with himself as secretary. Unlike the Indian Congress it was broad-based, not confined to an elite of intellectuals. Anyone could join for a modest fee, and the program called for nothing less than harmony between Europeans and Indians and self-help for the Indian community on a wide scale. Recruits came in quickly and the Congress set about hearing grievances, buttonholing the press, and teaching Indians to put aside some of the customs that Gandhi felt gave Europeans an excuse for discrimination, such as willingness to live in filth.

Gandhi now applied to practice law in the Supreme Court of Natal, and again, although his application was approved, he was reminded that he must remove his turban. This time, however, he complied, saying that the chief justice was entitled to lay down rules for his own courtroom, and that the turban issue was not important.

Gandhi's instincts about the seriousness of the voting legislation were soon confirmed, for the Natal government began trying to impose an annual tax of twenty-five pounds on every indentured laborer, considerably more than a laborer's yearly pay. The real intent was to drive the Indians back to India; where once they had been essential to the growth of South African commerce, now they were making their way into businesses the whites considered their own province and they were felt to be a threat to continued white dominance.

With the entire Indian community

behind him, Gandhi, by his writings and by appeals to the British authorities, succeeded in getting the tax reduced to three pounds—still a lot of money for a "coolie," but nevertheless a victory. He had less success with the voting law, which was modified only to the extent that the few Indians already on the voting list would not be excluded.

Gandhi spent the next two years organizing, protesting, and writing, meanwhile conducting a successful law practice. He raised the Indians' consciousness, but for several years could claim no particular successes. Nevertheless he persisted.

When he returned to India for a short stay in 1896 to get his family, he was already a figure of some minor public importance there. The South African question had received some attention in India, and Gandhi went about the country rousing public opinion as best he could. He also wrote a pamphlet cautiously stating the problem for Indians in South Africa—a pamphlet that was to cause him severe problems when he returned to South Africa.

Using Rajkot as his base, he moved about India speaking and meeting influential people. In Bombay he was asked to read a paper, but his old nervousness reappeared, and it had to be read for him. In Poona, though, he aroused the interest of two men who were to be of great importance for his future. One was G. K. Gokhale, a leader of the Indian independence movement and a man always looking for young adherents. The other was B.

G. Tilak, a jurist and mathematician as well as a reformer. Tilak was an advocate of "direct action" to achieve independence, a revolutionary; Gokhale believed that independence could be attained through constitutional means. Despite their differences, they sponsored a joint meeting in Poona to hear about the problems of Indians in South Africa. Gokhale took a great interest in Gandhi, and Gandhi turned to him in gratitude for advice on practical matters of politics from then on, both from South Africa and later when he returned to India permanently.

During his travels around India, Gandhi received a telegram from Dada Abdullah asking Gandhi to return in time for the Natal parliament's opening in January.

Gandhi and his family sailed for South Africa on November 30, 1896, aboard the S.S. *Courtland*—into a tempest.

The tempest arose from a brief report by Reuter's News Agency from London on Gandhi's pamphlet about the South African problem: "A pamphlet published in India declares that the Indians in Natal are robbed and assaulted and treated like beasts and are unable to obtain redress. The *Times of India* advocates an inquiry into these allegations." Gandhi, in fact, had written no such thing; his pamphlet was far more circumspect and reasoned even than his writings in South Africa, but the Natal papers picked up the incorrect dispatch, and when Gandhi's ship reached Durban, South African whites were up in arms.

Their peace of mind was not helped by the fact that the *Courtland* coincidentally arrived at Durban on the same day, December 19, as another ship from India, the S.S. *Naderi*. Dada Abdullah was the owner of one and agent for the other, and the ships carried a total of 800 Indians, half of them due to disembark in Natal. To the whites it seemed like an invasion, and the fact of the two ships' arriving on the same day smacked to them of conspiracy. They held a protest meeting and called on the government to keep the Indians from coming ashore. The usual quarantine was extended for many days as the government sought a solution. Indians were offered free passage back home; passengers were threatened, the shipowners were threatened. Finally, after twenty-three days, the ships were permitted to enter the harbor, and Gandhi, convinced that he should not sneak ashore, bravely walked through the angry crowds that had gathered. He was pelted with eggs and stones, and feared for his life. Just then, the wife of the superintendent of police, a Mrs. Alexander, happened by, recognized Gandhi as a friend of her husband's and escorted him through the white throng, using her open parasol to ward of missiles. The sight of a white woman with the little brown man stopped the crowd. At the home of a friend with whom he was to stay, Gandhi's wounds were dressed while a

Gandhi (third from right in middle row) with Indian Ambulance Corps during Boer War, 1899.

mob collected and threatened to burn down the house. This time it was the police superintendent who deterred the crowd while Gandhi, deciding that subterfuge was the better part of valor, slipped out of the house disguised as an Indian constable accompanied by a detective dressed as an Indian merchant. Thus was Gandhi welcomed back to South Africa on January 13, 1897.

Soon, however, the news reports were corrected, apologies were forthcoming, and the local press conceded that Gandhi's actions had been well within his rights. His reputation was further enhanced when he refused to prosecute the rowdies who had pelted him.

When the Boer War broke out in 1899, Gandhi's ambivalence about colonial rulers took a curious turn. The British Natal colony and the Boer Transvaal and Orange Free State regarded Indians as second-class citizens, but Gandhi felt that as long as he was working within the British system and trying to change it, he and other Indians owed a duty to the crown. He believed that the discrimination Indians encountered was only a perversion of British justice. Gandhi offered to recruit a thousand Indians for the British, who, although reluctant to have Indians serve as soldiers, agreed to let them form an. ambulance corps. The men served honorably, and Gandhi and his followers felt that with this gesture their troubles with the English of South Africa would be over. They were wrong, of course.

But it was in this fit of euphoria that in October 1901 Gandhi turned over conduct of the Natal Indian Congress to associates, packed his family (there were now two more sons, Ramdas and Devadas) and sailed for India again, this time he believed permanently, to set up law practice in Bombay and enter Indian politics. He attended a Congress meeting in December in Calcutta, introduced a resolution in support of the Indians of South Africa, renewed his close friendship with Gokhale, and resumed traveling around the country—third-class, in the conviction that one could not work for the poor unless one lived like them. Despite these activities, he became disillusioned with Indian politics, realizing that with the British as powerful as ever, Indian Congress meetings and Indian politics tended to be window dressing.

Rescue came in the form of an urgent request from his Natal compatriots, who had extracted a promise from him that he would return if they needed him within a year. This time he returned without his family to find that the Boer War had changed nothing; the British had control now of Boer territory, but they were not about to fulfill the pledges they had made to redress Indian grievances. The immediate occasion for the request for his return was a visit to South Africa by British Colonial Secretary Joseph Chamberlain. Gandhi met him and presented the list of Indian grievances. Chamberlain said he would look into the situation, but explained blandly that of course London could not dictate to Natal.

The situation was as bad as ever, and Gandhi saw he would have to remain in Africa. He sent for his family and quickly established a thriving law practice in Johannesburg, in the Transvaal, where the restrictions against Indians were worse than in Natal.

While still in Durban, Gandhi had decided to start a newspaper, which he called *Indian Opinion*. Although he did not technically own it, he provided most of the money for it and controlled it, in addition to writing editorials for it. When he moved to Johannesburg he prevailed upon a newfound English friend, Albert West, who operated a printing shop, to take charge of running *Indian Opinion*.

Other European friends were drawn into his inner circle and were to be mainstays of his battles during his remaining years in South Africa. One was Herman Kallenbach, a wealthy Polish-born architect who had grown up in Germany and who could build anything. Another was Henry Polak, the young English-born editor of a Transvaal political weekly. There was also Sonja Schlesin, of Russian origin, who like Polak and Kallenbach was a nonpracticing Jew. Another important non-Indian colleague was Charles Freer Andrews, an English missionary whom Gokhale had recommended to Gandhi to aid in the struggle.

It was Polak who brought to Gandhi's attention John Ruskin's *Unto This Last*, which in effect demanded that the rich should place their wealth at the service of the community, especially the poor. Gandhi found in the book principles that fit into his own and from which he would never deviate: that the good of the individual is contained in the good of all; that all work has the same value; that a life of labor as a farmer or craftsman is the best life.

The idea of a simple laboring community took hold in Gandhi's mind (influenced perhaps by a visit to a Trappist monastery where he admired the monks' quiet industry), and he set about founding such a community where *Indian Opinion* would be the village industry, at least at the start. In 1904, therefore, Gandhi bought a piece of farmland outside Durban, at a place called Phoenix, and so Phoenix Farm, the first of Gandhi's self-contained communities—or *ashrams*—in South Africa and India was born, supported by the substantial earnings of Gandhi as a successful Johannesburg lawyer, who would visit whenever he could, taking along some Johannesburg friends and family.

All the main elements of Gandhi's personal and public life had now been set in place, except for one, and it took another war to settle this one. This war, a relatively small one, involved a Zulu uprising in 1906. Again Gandhi felt it his duty to support the British; and he raised a noncombatant corps of twenty-four stretcher-bearers, but most of their work consisted of tending Zulu wounded, whom the white South Africans would leave to die. This experience of brutality and indifference deeply affected Gandhi, and he

Members of the Phoenix Settlement, Natal, 1906. Gandhi is fourth from left, middle row of white-clothed men. Kasturba is fifth from left in row of women below.

determined to spend the rest of his life serving humanity. To this end, he felt, one had to forgo all personal pleasure and indulgence, including sex. Therefore, with a long tradition of Hindu holy-man celibacy to support him, he decided to adopt *brahmacharya*—permanent celibacy—as one of the tenets of faith, along with *ahimsa*, nonviolence to all living things, and *satyagraha*, the force of truth and love, his own invention. He consulted with his friends, made his

decision, and informed Kasturba of it. She did not argue.

Thus, many years before he returned to India, his course was firmly set. Although he would modify them constantly, and was forever finding new applications and new definitions, these were the three cornerstones of his life.

He was soon to have a field of action on which to test his principles. On August 9, 1905, the Natal Legislative Council passed a poll-tax bill aimed primarily at Indians, and initial attempts to oppose it came to naught. Then in August 1906 the Transvaal published the Asiatic Law Amendment Ordinance, requiring all Indians over the age of eight to be fingerprinted and to carry with them at all times a registration certificate. Anyone refusing would forfeit his right to stay in the Transvaal and could be fined, imprisoned, or deported. The certificate would have to be shown to get any government service or even a bicycle license. Gandhi feared that the Transvaal bill would be imitated throughout the rest of South Africa if it were adopted, and he objected fiercely to treating Indians as criminals by requiring fingerprinting.

On September 11, 1906, an Indian

Settlers at Tolstoy Farm, 1910. Gandhi (left) and Herman Kallenbach sit at the center of the middle row.

Gandhi and Kasturba in 1913.

mass meeting was held at the Empire Theater in Johannesburg at which three thousand Indians present called for withdrawal of the registration bill. Gandhi's hand was evident in the fact that all the two dozen or so speakers called for passive resistance to fight the ordinance. Gandhi, in his speech, called for everyone to pledge not to be fingerprinted and not to carry the registration card.

Since the bill had not yet formally become law, Gandhi and an associate were dispatched to London to plead with Lord Elgin, who was then colonial secretary. There, they sent out press releases, called on legislators, and in general made as much noise as possible. They got a sympathetic hearing and on the way back to South Africa learned that Lord Elgin had withheld approval of the ordinance. But on January 1, 1907, the Transvaal was granted self-government, and the British government could not interfere, so the bill became law in March and took effect July 1.

Gandhi and his colleagues mounted picket lines and conducted a nonviolent campaign to persuade every Indian to refuse to register. The government deadline was extended several times in the face of this general strike. The consequences were inevitable: scores of Indians were arrested, tried, and imprisoned, including Gandhi, who got his first taste of prison in January 1908. He served about two weeks of a two-month sentence, and learned that prison could be a useful place to relax and read, while still managing to keep in touch with other *satyagrahis*.

His principal weapon was civil resistance, which to him meant not passively accepting injustice but actively, although nonviolently, opposing it by openly breaking the law and willingly suffering the penalty for doing so.

His release from prison came after he accepted a promise by General Jan Christiaan Smuts, a Boer leader who was cooperating with the British, that the registration ordinance would be repealed as soon as the Indians had complied; that in effect it was all pro forma. Gandhi took him at his word, although some Indians felt he had betrayed them, and nothing happened. The law stayed on the books.

On August 16, 1908, two thousand Indians in Johannesburg gathered at a monster rally and burned their registration certificates. It was an act heard 'round the world; the *London Daily Mail* compared it to the Boston Tea Party. And the resistance continued, with *satyagrahis* finding nonviolent ways to court arrest and imprisonment; it became a mark of honor to go to prison. On one day almost a quarter of the Transvaal's Indians were in prison.

On October 7, 1908, Gandhi was arrested again and served two months. At the beginning of 1909 he was jailed once again, this time for three months. Released, he sailed for London to be present as the union of the South African colonies was negotiated. Again there were sympathetic hearings from the English, but no substantive change in the Indians' conditions.

In 1910, seeing the need for a place of refuge, especially for families of *satyagrahis* who were in prison, Gandhi established another *ashram*, which he called Tolstoy Farm, an 1100-acre farm donated by Kallenbach. It was twenty-one miles from Johannesburg and Gandhi was able to spend a great deal of time there, even to keep his family there. He often got up at 2:00 a.m. and walked the twenty-

one miles to his office in Johannesburg. The *satyagrahis* grew their own food, educated their children, and made their own furniture and clothing. The farm, which had a number of children, also provided a convenient testing ground for Gandhi's theories about education and diet, and he started his practice of regular fasts to sharpen his moral sense.

In 1912, at Gandhi's urging, Gokhale toured South Africa for five weeks with Gandhi as his guide. Gokhale got assurances from South African authorities that discriminatory laws would be repealed, but again these assurances came to nothing.

Then, in March 1913 in a test case, the Supreme Court ruled that Hindu, Moslem, and Parsi marriages were invalid, and Indian wives were in effect concubines without status, liable to deportation, and that their children were illegitimate. This ultimate insult touched off a new wave of protest in which even Kasturba, normally in the background, took part. One group of women marched illegally from the Transvaal into the Natal coalfields and persuaded Indian miners to walk off their jobs in protest. The mineowners, already in trouble with white miners, were dumbfounded by the Indian walkout, which was unheard of. Women were arrested; strikers left their homes and marched off into an unknown pilgrimage, living in the open, with dedicated *satyagrahis* offering help along the way. It was decided that the strikers and other protesters should head for Tolstoy Farm, as the only practical place to

care for them. The jails were filled to overflowing, Gandhi was imprisoned again. Fifty thousand indentured laborers took up the cause and walked off their jobs. Phoenix Farm became a haven. *Satyagrahis* were put to hard labor in prison, and some died, including women.

On December 18, 1913, Gandhi was released, and at a meeting in Durban he appeared in the *dhoti*—the traditional Indian garb that he was to wear for the rest of his life. His feet were bare.

In January white railway workers struck on their own. In a masterstroke, Gandhi declared that the Indians would not take advantage of the government's difficulties to make things worse. He called off the *satyagraha* campaign. The impact was electrifying, and praise flowed in from England and India. Even South African whites were impressed. Gandhi's moral ascendance was complete.

After intense pressure from the British envoy in India and from the British cabinet, the three-pound tax on Indians was rescinded, as were strictures against Indian marriages and elements of the indentured labor system. Gandhi negotiated the agreement with Smuts, this time as an equal.

Gandhi's work in South Africa was done. The blueprint for the future had been drawn. Although Indians never became first-class citizens of South Africa—and still aren't—there was nothing left for Gandhi to do. His next horizon beckoned: India.

Gandhi as a *satyagrahi* in South Africa.

Return to Home

On January 19, 1915, Gandhi returned to India, landing in Bombay, where he was greeted as the hero of Indian struggles in South Africa. He was not sure what he would do next, although it was clear his future lay in public service. His family had preceded him while he was visiting in London. Gandhi joined his family at Santiniketan, the commual school in Bengal that had been founded by the poet Rabindranath Tagore, who had recently won the Nobel prize for literature. The visit was arranged by Charles Andrews, a colleague of Gandhi's from South Africa, who taught at the school.

Tagore and Gandhi could not have been more unlike, though each recognized in the other the stamp of greatness, and it was Tagore who soon dubbed Gandhi "Mahatma," or Great Soul, a traditional Indian honorary title by which Gandhi became known throughout the world. Tagore had no taste for Gandhi's ascetic temper and was disturbed by what he regarded as Gandhi's streak of violence. For Tagore the science and culture of the West were admirable things to be embraced, while Gandhi, although admiring much in western culture, was marching toward a rejection of western influence as detrimental to India.

Even Gandhi's obssession with food and diet found no sympathy in the poet, who loved fine, rich foods. Once, when Gandhi objected that bread fried in oil was like poison, Tagore replied that it must be a very slow poison, as he had been eating it all his life and it hadn't harmed him yet.

Shortly after Gandhi's arrival at the school Tagore left on a trip, and Gandhi immediately tried to reshape the school to his own standards. He called on the 125 students and staff, who lived in a dreamy existence of art and poetry, to do their own cooking, to clean their own latrines, and to dispense with servants, much as he and his followers had done at Phoenix Farm and Tolstoy Farm. The persuasive Gandhi brought the students round, although even the faithful Andrews argued against trying to bring these practices to the school. Gandhi's success was short-lived; when he left a few weeks later, the students—without protest from Tagore—reverted to their usual ways. The only vestige of Gandhi's stay was an annual celebration thereafter known as Gandhi day, when the students and staff gave the servants the day off and did their own chores.

Taking Gokhale's advice, Gandhi stayed out of politics for the time being, traveling about the country,

Gandhi and Kasturba upon their return to India in 1915.
At left, Gandhi photographed at the same time.

meeting people, taking the measure of his native land. But he spoke wherever he went, and usually found himself the object of veneration, with crowds seeking his blessing or even just the sight of him.

Once, he attended a sacred bathing ceremony—along with thousands of others—at Hardwar, only to come away angered by the hypocrisy and filth he saw. Typically, he decided to atone personally for the transgressions of others by imposing new restrictions on his life-style. He vowed never to eat more than five articles of food in any twenty-four hours—a vow he kept to the end of his life.

Since he had decided to stay out of politics for the moment, his first speeches and writings concentrated on reform of men and of society—but in moral rather than political terms. He had decided not to practice law anymore, but to devote himself to spreading the concepts of *ahimsa*, *brahmacharya*, and *satyagraha*. For this, he concluded, he needed an *ashram* like Phoenix Farm and Tolstoy Farm where he and his followers could practice and preach his ideals. A number of offers for him to set up an *ashram* were received from around the country and he finally accepted an offer by a group of friends in Ahmadabad—mostly wealthy businessmen—to establish his *ashram* there, ultimately at a site on the Sabarmati River.

Almost immediately after its founding in May 1915 the *ashram* was confronted by a crisis over the issue of untouchability. For centuries the caste system of India had relegated to the fringes of society those who did the menial, distasteful tasks of life. These outcastes were, because of their low station in life, felt to be literally untouchable by others, who believed they would be made unclean by physical contact. Under the doctrine of *karma*, a person's condition is the natural and deserved result of his conduct in previous lives. The outcastes were doomed, generation after generation, to the lowest, most abject tasks, such as gathering ordure from the streets, and were barred from walking where others walked and from entering temples.

Acceptance of untouchability was almost universal, even among the Untouchables, but Gandhi saw this as one of the principal blights of Hinduism and of India, and beginning at the *ashram* he fought against it throughout his life. When he decided that the *ashram* must have at least a symbolic, token Untouchable family in it, his financial backers withdrew support, and even Kasturba objected, believing that contact with Untouchables was demeaning and unthinkable.

In his autobiography Gandhi describes the situation this way.

"Their admission created a flutter among the friends who had been helping the *ashram*. The first difficulty was found with regard to the use of the well. The man in charge of the water lift objected that drops of water from our bucket would pollute him. All monetary help was stopped. My wife and other women did not seem quite

Gandhi and Kasturba, seated center, at a reception in Ahmadabad, 1915.

to relish the admission of the Untouchable friends. In the beginning we proclaimed to the world that the *ashram* would not countenance untouchability."

Gandhi brought everyone in the *ashram* around to his point of view, but the money problem seemed insoluble. Then, in one of those providential occurrences that he

always believed would come along, a wealthy patron drove up to the *ashram* one day and simply dropped off enough money for it to continue.

Gandhi had not returned to an India that was totally somnolent; it was merely awaiting his call to action. There had been stirrings, although long years of subservience to the British were hard to shake off.

The reasons for the stirrings were not just that the British ruled, but the way they ruled. Hundreds of millions of Indians were at the mercy of a system dominated by some one thousand Britons at the top of the Indian civil service. These men lived extraordinarily luxurious lives, but never became part of the country they were ruling. And just as individual Englishmen used India as a place to make reputations and fine livings, so the empire used India to fill its treasury. Although the people of India were usually close to starvation, British traders were permitted to export huge quantities of food for sale at high profits elsewhere. It has been calculated that the British took out of India nearly half the country's net revenue, the better to maintain living standards in Britain and to keep the rest of the British empire afloat.

Unlike previous invaders and conquerors throughout Indian history, the British were not absorbed into the mainstream, but deliberately remained aloof, outside, imperious, determined to enforce a sense of their cultural superiority. One means of maintaining their rule was to divide the native population, particularly to make sure that Hindus and Moslems were at odds. Besides maintaining many princely states, whose rulers or maharajas were in effect co-opted into the imperial rule, the British in the middle of the nineteenth century deliberately arranged that the Moslems, although only 20 percent of the population, made up some 40 percent of the army. This could not help but rankle the Hindu population, since the army was one of the stepping-stones to a slightly better life. The British also devised schemes to benefit rich Indian landowners at the expense of small farmers, further co-opting the wealthy.

In the middle of the nineteenth century there had been various Indian associations that attempted to open a dialogue with the British on the problems of the Indian population. Finally, in 1885 the Indian National Congress was formed, initially with the intention of trying to make the British aware of the problems. But years of memo writing and resolutions had produced no response, and by the turn of the century the Congress had become a broad-based political party dedicated to home rule. Although Gokhale, as a leader of the Congress, had sharply criticized the British (especially after an outbreak of plague and famine had been ignored by the

Gandhi and Kasturba during their first visit to Madras, 1915. M. Y. Hasan (left) and G. A. Natesan stand behind them.

Gandhi (seated far right in carriage) being led in a procession through Karachi, 1916.

British), and had been thrown in jail for seven years as a result, when Gandhi returned to India the Congress, despite calls for home rule, basically sought solutions within the framework of British hegemony. In addition, in typical Indian fashion, the idea of violent action was ruled out, making things much easier for the British.

In this Congress of educated—often British-educated—upper-class Indians, however, stirrings were beginning to be felt. A few months before the outbreak of World War I, Annie Besant, an English Indiaphile as well as Theosophist, told an audience in London that the price of India's loyalty in the war was India's freedom. In India itself, where she was more Indian than the Indians, she founded in September 1916 the Home Rule League, and struck fear into the hearts of the British.

Mrs. Besant had also founded the Central Hindu College in Benares in 1892, and in 1916 it formally became a university. At the ceremony marking the occasion, on February 6, Gandhi was among the notables asked to speak. Sharing the platform with elaborately attired maharajas, educators, and other eminent persons, he proceeded to attack the British, the use of the English language, Hinduism, wealth, the filth of the Indian temples and railroads—not the sort of thing everyone present expected to hear on this festive occasion.

"I do venture to suggest," he began, "that we have now reached almost the end of our resources in speechmaking. I wanted to say it is a matter of deep humiliation and shame for us that I am compelled to address my countrymen in a language that is foreign to me. The charge against us is that we have no initiative. How can we have any if we are to devote the precious years of our life to the mastery of a foreign tongue? Suppose we had been receiving education through our vernaculars, what should we have today? We should have today a free India.

"The Congress has passed a resolution about self-government, but no paper contribution will ever give us self-government. No amount of speeches will ever make us fit for self-government. Is it right that the lanes of our sacred temple should be as dirty as they are? If even our temples are not models of roominess and cleanliness, what can our self-government be? We do not know the elementary laws of cleanliness. We spit anywhere.

"The maharaja who presided yesterday spoke about the poverty of India, but what did we witness? A most gorgeous show, an exhibition of jewelry which made a spendid feast for the eyes of the greatest jeweler who chose to come from Paris. I feel like saying to those noblemen: 'There is no salvation for India unless you strip yourselves of this jewelry and hold it in trust for your countrymen in India.' "

As he went on in this vein, the audience, as well as the notables sharing the platform, became more and more restive. "We shall never be granted self-government," Gandhi said, still speaking in the almost monotonous tones he always used in speaking in public. "Look at the history of the British empire and the British nation; freedom-loving as it is, it will not be a party to give freedom to a people who will not take it themselves."

At this point, some people on the platform got up to leave, even as others in the audience called for him to go on, and in the uproar he was unable to finish. Gandhi now received invitations from all over the country to speak, but after this one outburst he persisted in speaking about morality and the evils of coffee drinking, and there was little of politics. His speeches tended to be diffuse and unfocused.

In 1917 a big turning point came in a place so remote that Gandhi had never heard of it. But it changed the thrust of his life and thereby the future of India. Just as a particular law or indignity had become the focus for his *satyagraha* in South Africa, so the mundane indigo plant and a place called Champaran became the sparks that ignited his career and the march to Indian independence, a march that included repeated nonviolent, noncooperation campaigns, fasts, and imprisonment.

Champaran and Beyond

**Gandhi in 1918
during Kheda
satyagraha.**

andhi was on the fringes of the Indian National Congress in Lucknow in December 1916. He lived in his own tent and was an eccentric figure, with his huge white turban and white clothing, among the Western-attired delegates. As Gandhi told it; "I must confess that I did not then know even the name, much less the geographical position of, Champaran, and I had hardly any notion of indigo plantations." So it was with some impatience that he listened to a man named Rajkumar Shukla importune him about the plight of indigo-farming peasants in Champaran. Shukla had, with no success at all, been buttonholing much more important delegates than Gandhi, and his turning to Gandhi was as much happenstance as anything; Shukla needed an ear, someone to listen to him and to act. Gandhi could barely understand Shukla's language, the Bihari dialect, and certainly not the point Shukla was trying to make.

Shukla eventually brought an interpreter to Gandhi's tent, a lawyer named Brajkishore Prasad. Gandhi, thinking Prasad was merely an exploiter of the poor peasants, took an instant dislike to him, which was to change later. Despite the intercession of Prasad, Gandhi was inclined not to take the whole matter too seriously,

Gandhi's home at his *ashram* at Sabarmati.

63

and suggested that Shukla and Prasad put their case before the Congress. They did so, but the Congress promptly proposed that the matter of the peasants' rights be referred to a government commission, a sure road to nowhere.

Shukla was not satisfied and continued to pester Gandhi, following him to Kanpur and then to the Sabarmati *ashram*. He was a determined man, and Gandhi finally agreed to visit Champaran.

After some missed signals, the pair arrived in the area looking like a couple of dirt-poor peasants, although Gandhi certainly wasn't and Shukla, who had been an active agitator in the region for several years, had some education and property.

The situation facing Gandhi involved planters, mostly Europeans, who had leased land from local owners, and tenant farmers who under feudal-type local agreements were required to plant a certain percentage of their land to indigo, the plant from which blue dye was made. Under a system that had been in effect for more than a century, the indigo crop had to be paid as rent, which meant that the landholders were crediting the tenant farmers with only a fraction of what the crop was really worth.

The current crisis had had its origins in the early years of the century, when German industry perfected a synthetic blue dye, making indigo superfluous.

Gandhi's own room at the Sabarmati *ashram*.

The demand for indigo collapsed, but not the landlords' desire for profits. To replace the no longer profitable indigo crop the landlords simply imposed higher taxes and rents, and peasants were beaten, cheated, and kept in abject poverty under a British government that looked away and in fact was a handmaiden to the landlords. While some Indian landowners engaged in the same practices, it was the British, with their far greater influence on government, who were the principal offenders.

The peasants had been trying unsuccessfully to counter the new rents and other oppressive measures with lawsuits, and many a lawyer found this a lucrative practice. Gandhi roamed the area with Shukla and other local people, especially lawyers, learning about the indigo problem, seeing the poverty, absorbing the misery of the peasants. Word spread quickly through the region that a savior had come to help the peasants.

Gandhi quickly came up with a plan so unheard of, so revolutionary, so unexpected, yet so ostensibly low-key, that neither the lawyers nor the planters nor the British authorities knew quite what it meant or how to react.

First of all, said Gandhi, the idea of further lawsuits was to be dropped since litigation would only enrich lawyers; this, to a group made up in large part of lawyers! Second, the lawyers should put aside their practices and go out into the countryside and collect evidence—huge amounts of evidence—of the inequities

and injustices being foisted on the peasants. The lawyers, he said, should act only as unpaid clerks, as he himself would do, gathering personal testimony about the situation. They and he would have to face the possibility of going to jail. The goal of the campaign, he concluded, was to free the peasants from fear; everything else would follow.

And so it did, but not without some detours and government opposition. The planters, seeing how day by day Gandhi's fame was spreading throughout the region, tried to get this outside agitator to leave. The government was not sure what to do, and temporarily left Gandhi alone. But on April 16, as Gandhi made his way to a village on an elephant ("an elephant, by the way, is as about as common in Champaran as a bullock cart in Gujarat," he wrote later) to investigate a report that a peasant had been mistreated, a policeman rode up on a bicycle and served Gandhi with a notice to leave Champaran. It was an invitation to *satyagraha*. Gandhi reports: "I wrote to the effect that I did not propose to comply with it and leave Champaran till my inquiry was finished. Thereupon I received a summons to take my trial the next day for disobeying the order to leave Champaran."

The scene the next day in the town of Motihari struck fear into the British. Peasants by the thousands had arrived in the town, not, as one biographer put it, to welcome a man who represented Congress, or a man known as a politician or a reformer; rather, "the confrontation of Mahatma and peasantry was a purely Messianic moment. God had descended in their midst to destroy unrighteousness."

The local magistrate seemed to have some sense of the occasion, and sought nervously to duck the issue, in which Gandhi was accused of being a disturber of the peace. The government pressed the magistrate to postpone the case, but Gandhi demurred, saying he wanted to plead guilty, but that his only motive in coming to Champaran was to get the facts.

He then stated a basic tenet of *satyagraha*: "The only safe and honorable course for a self-respecting man is to do what I have decided to do, that is, to submit without protest to the penalty of disobedience . . . not for want of respect for lawful authority, but in obedience to the higher law of our being, the voice of conscience."

The nonplused magistrate sought to temporize, saying he would render a judgment after a two-hour recess. He called on Gandhi to put up bail for the two hours. Gandhi declined. In befuddlement and anxiety, the magistrate—noting the buzzing of the angry peasants who crowded the courtroom and the streets—released Gandhi without bail. A cheer went up. Gandhi was free to pursue his fact-finding mission.

Help came from around the country as students and others turned up to do their part. Thousands of depositions were taken over half a year—all to provide irrefutable evidence of the planters' exploitative tactics—and finally the government ordered a commission set up with Gandhi as a member to decide what should be done. The depositions made the outcome easily predictable; the only question was what the planters would have to pay in recompense. Gandhi proposed a 50 percent refund on illegally obtained taxes and other payments; the planters offered 25 percent. Gandhi readily agreed to the lower figure, saying the amount was unimportant, that the principle that had been won was the important thing. And indeed it was, for the power of the raj, the power of the government and the English settlers, was shown to be subject to the power of the Indian masses. The great *satyagraha* movement had been set in motion, and for the next fifteen years Gandhi held a central place in the politics of reform and independence, years that would make Gandhi a household name around the world and a familiar figure in the newspapers and newsreels of the time. He was the Mahatma.

Gandhi stayed on in Champaran for some months to follow up the economic victory with an educational campaign aimed at teaching the farmers tenets of cleanliness and self-help and was making some headway (as usual, the farmers slipped back into their old ways soon after he left) when he received a request to help some textile millworkers in their fight for a cost-of-living bonus to help counter the soaring prices that followed an outbreak of the plague in the region near the *ashram*. The request came from Anasuyabehn, sister of Ambalae

Mohandas K. Gandhi.

Sarabhai, the biggest textile manufacturer in Ahmadabad and the man who had dropped off the money for the *ashram* after its Untouchable crisis. Sarabhai himself seemed to welcome Gandhi's intercession. Gandhi—by then besides being called Mahatma he was being addressed as Gandhiji, the *-ji* suffix being another honorific—arranged for arbitration, but negotiations broke down and work stoppages erupted. The workers were seeking a 50 percent increase; the owners offered 20 percent. Gandhi proposed a compromise at 35 percent, but the owners balked, and on February 22, 1918, declared a lockout.

Gandhi called on the workers to meet the owners' intransigence with steadfast pledges not to return to work unless their demands were met, even though they had few resources to maintain them in a strike. He also demanded of them adherence to the concept of nonviolence, no matter what the provocation.

Day after day Gandhi met with the workers, exhorted them to remain firm and to accept suffering if they were to win. Anasuyabehn blithely collected money and found jobs for the workers, even as her brother and other owners organized strikebreakers. But privation and weakness were thinning the ranks of the strikers, and some started to drift away. Gandhi therefore declared he would fast until the strike was settled or until all the strikers left the mills for good. The vow startled not only the strikers but also the millowners, many of whom were among Gandhi's supporters and admirers. After three days the owners and strikers settled for 35 percent.

At the same time there was a dispute between peasants and the government in the Kheda district near Ahmadabad. The peasants said the weather had caused the crop yield to drop by 25 percent and that they should not have to pay their assessment. The government disputed the claim and demanded that the taxes be paid. Gandhi arranged a compromise whereby the richer peasants would pay while the poorer ones did not.

With Champaran, Ahmadabad, and Kheda, Gandhi's apprenticeship in *satyagraha* was over. Only a national test remained, and, typically, it was the British who touched it off.

Hartal and Amritsar

After World War I and the gallant service of thousands of Indian troops, there was a general feeling among Indian leaders that the British were prepared to accede to Indian demands for home rule. In August 1917 the British secretary of state read in the House of Commons a statement declaring that the government looked toward "the increasing association of Indians in every branch of the administration, and the gradual development of self-governing institutions, with a view to the progressive realization of responsible government in India as an integral part of the empire." While this did not say flatly that India would achieve self-governing status like Canada, most Indians took it to mean just that.

However, the top-ranking members of the Indian civil service (those one thousand imperial rulers) opposed the idea and did everything to sabotage its implementation. One of their moves was to prove the final blow. The British Indian government set up a committee to decide how to deal with increased Indian agitation for home rule (Tilak had been put in jail again). The committee, led by an English judge, Sir Sidney Rowlatt, recommended that judges should be allowed to try political cases without juries and that political suspects could be jailed without due process. The British Indian rulers happily accepted the recommendations and the Rowlatt Acts were passed on March 18, 1919, adding to the other imperial laws already on the books, such as the power to prohibit large political gatherings.

Gandhi called for a *hartal*, or national strike, on March 30 as a protest. He did not directly call it a strike, but rather a day of fasting and prayer. Of course, if one fasted and prayed all day, one could not work. Congress leaders held back, not knowing what to make of the call.

But the populace did. Gandhi was by now a figure of great moral authority and with a religious aura particularly loved by Hindus, and his voice was heard throughout the land.

On March 30 in Delhi, and on April 6 in the rest of the country, *hartal* was observed. There were huge demonstrations in which Hindus and Moslems fraternized as they marched through the streets. The police opened fire in some areas, killing nine people in Delhi. Economic life came to a halt. In Bombay Gandhi addressed a crowd at a mosque and he and other leaders peacefully sold seditious papers and prohibited books. Gandhi started publishing a paper that existed only to be illegal, and sent a copy to the police commissioner with a note pointing out

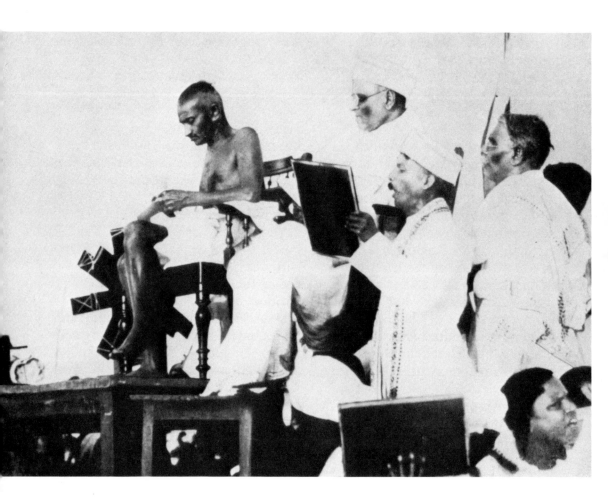

**Gandhi addresses a meeting in Madras, 1925. S. S. Iyengar
sits to his left.**

that it was illegal. But while this active if peaceful protest was going on, violence broke out elsewhere. Gandhi was prevented from traveling to Delhi, and it was reported—incorrectly—that he had been arrested; the reports led to arson, sabotage, and general rowdiness. Gandhi deplored the violence and called for an end to the *hartal*, but the violence continued.

In Amritsar, a city in the Punjab, it came to a climax. On April 10 an English woman, a schoolteacher, was assaulted. The city had been the scene of the worst violence. On the eleventh, British General Reginald E. H. Dyer arrived and proclaimed a ban on public meetings. But on the thirteenth, thousands of Indians gathered for a protest meeting at the Jallianwallah Bagh, either in defiance of the ban or in ignorance of it. Jallianwallah Bagh had originally been a walled garden (*bagh* means "garden"), but now it was merely an enclosed square with high walls and several narrow entrances. Without further warning General Dyer led about a hundred troops—all Indians, Gurkhas, and Baluchis—and an armored weapons car to the square. The armored car could not get through the narrow opening into the square, so Dyer led his men in and ordered them to fire carefully into the crowd of men, women, and children, making each bullet count. For ten minutes the soldiers fired, taking aim with each shot. The trapped crowd tried to clamber up the walls or to squeeze out through the narrow entrances. There was chaos. Some women with children in their arms jumped into a well to escape the bullets. When all the bullets had been expended—1650 rounds according to a later report—the firing stopped. The official police report later said that 379 people had been killed and over a thousand wounded. Almost every shot had indeed counted.

The general's intention had been clear and he told a board of inquiry later that he wanted to inflict enough death and blood to make sure the whole country knew it could not trifle with the British. He imposed martial law on the city and ordered all Indians to crawl on all fours when passing along the street where the English schoolteacher had been attacked. Because of martial law and strict censorship, it was some weeks before news of the massacre became widely known. Dyer was relieved of his command as London expressed shock and dismay over the massacre, but a public subscription raised thousands of

From left, Annie Besant, S. Sastri, Gandhi and Satyamurthi.

pounds, permitting him to retire to a life of ease. Gandhi was horrified at the bloodshed and called for a *satyagraha* campaign. In November he visited Amritsar with Charles Andrews and was mobbed by ecstatic Indians as he walked into the Golden Temple of the Sikhs.

In reponse to Amritsar, Gandhi called for a massive policy of noncooperation, boycotts of British goods, of British schools, even of British government jobs. But some conciliatory moves by the British again gave the appearance of progress, and he called off the campaign. "To trust is a virtue," he said. Other Indians, including Congress leaders and such Moslem leaders as Mohammed Ali Jinnah, were not as optimisitic, and in the interest of Moslem-Hindu unity Gandhi in June 1920 called once more for noncooperation. This time he accompanied his words with a symbolic action: he returned two medals he had received in South Africa. He wrote to the British viceroy saying: "I can retain neither respect nor affection for a government which has been moving from wrong to wrong

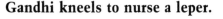

Gandhi kneels to nurse a leper.

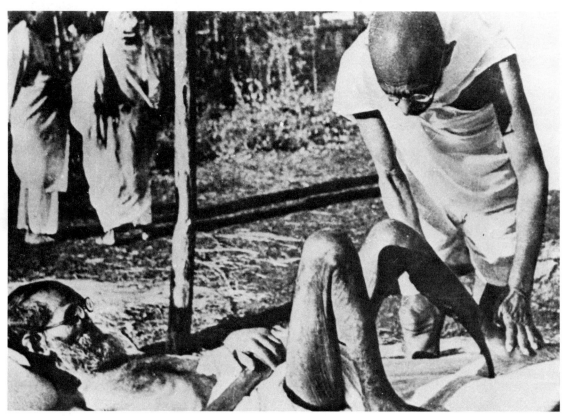

in order to defend its immorality." The action seemed to mark his final move to a complete break with his past respect for the British and his belief that he could work within the system. His call was heeded around the country: students left their classrooms, peasants refused to pay taxes, wealthy lawyers gave up their British-related practices. Gandhi traveled again around the country preaching noncooperation. The Congress had endorsed his call, and it was official Indian policy not to cooperate with the British.

As Gandhi moved about the country, Indians by the hundreds of thousands poured out to greet him—not even to listen to him speak, because mass rallies in those days did not have the benefit of microphones. They came just to see him, to be in his presence, to receive his *darshan*—vision of his sanctity. Just as he had drawn people of all backgrounds to him in South Africa, so now the millions were drawn to him. Gandhi was not at ease with this adulation. Though his popularity was essential to his politics, yet he felt that people should not be kissing his feet or worshiping him, but rather following in his footsteps.

An important element of the noncooperation movement was the call to boycott British cloth. Gandhi called on Indians not to wear foreign clothing, citing himself as an example. And he would call at rallies for everyone to strip off clothing made abroad and throw it into a pile to which he then set a match. He called on everyone to spin and weave their own clothing and again set an example by spinning each day. On July 31, 1921, Gandhi presided over a huge bonfire of foreign-made cloth in Bombay. He wore homemade rough *khadi* cloth as a sort of elongated diaper, sometimes with a white shawl in addition. It was this image of the spindly-legged little brown man in a *dhoti* that became the image of Gandhi around the world. Within India, likewise, the image of the Mahatma garbed in a *dhoti* became universally loved and revered, not only because of Gandhi's politics but because of his carrying out in practice his preachings about poverty, humility, and goodwill. To the Indians his voluntary assumption of poverty and homemade garb was a sign of his ultimate sainthood.

In November 1921 the prince of Wales visited India, touching off riots in Bombay and other areas—riots to which the British responded with forcible dispersion of meetings, midnight searches, and imprisonment. By January 1922, thirty thousand Congress workers had been imprisoned. The next month, under pressure for a wider mass civil disobedience campaign, Gandhi asked the peasants in Bardoli, in Gujarat State, to refuse to pay the land tax. The campaign started peacefully, but many miles away, in the little village of Chauri Chaura, a march of Gandhi's followers provoked the police, who abused the marchers. The demonstrators chased the policemen back into the station house and then set fire to the building, forcing the

Gandhi in Darjeeling, 1925. In center, behind Gandhi, is C. R. Das.

who died a few days later.

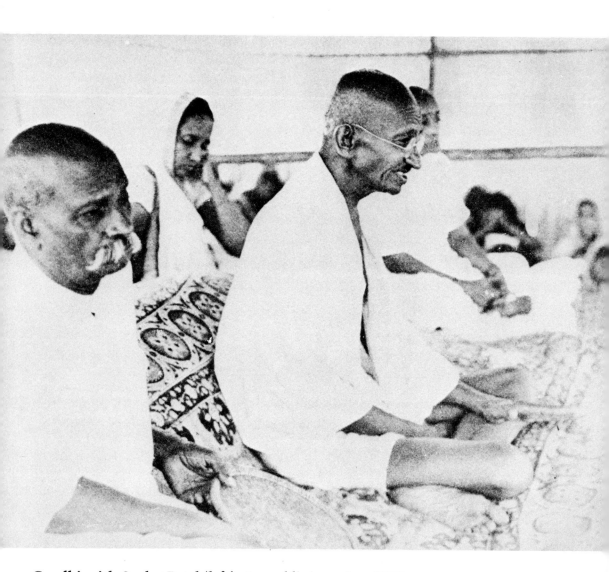

Gandhi with Sardar Patel (left) at a public meeting, 1929.

policemen out. As the policemen fled choking from the burning building they were set upon by the marchers and hacked to pieces. Gandhi promptly called off the civil disobedience campaign.

In one of those actions peculiar to British of the era, the authorities responded to Gandhi's calling off the campaign by arresting him. The police came for him at the Sabarmati *ashram* on the evening of March 10 and took him to prison. Gandhi welcomed his arrest, feeling his absence would help to restore order. The official charge was the writing of three seditious articles in Gandhi's weekly paper, *Young India*. In one of these articles he had said that the Viceroy, Lord Reading, "must clearly understand that the noncooperators are at war with the government. The strength of a noncooperator lies in his going to jail uncomplainingly. This is a fight to the finish. It is a conflict between the reign of violence and of public opinion. Those who are fighting for the latter are determined to submit to any violence rather than surrender their opinion."

The trial on March 18 was an extraordinary affair, with Judge Broomfield bowing respectfully to the prisoner, who was attired as usual in his loincloth. Gandhi nonplused the judge and the courtroom with his statement, in which he declared, among other things, his willingness to submit to the harshest penalty that could be given:

"I believe that I have rendered a service to India and England by showing in noncooperation the way out of the unnatural state in which both are living. In my humble opinion, noncooperation with evil is as much a duty as is cooperation with good. I am here, therefore, to invite and submit cheerfully to the highest penalty that can be inflicted upon me for what in law is a deliberate crime and what appears to me to be the highest duty of a citizen. The only course open to you, the judge, is either to resign your post and thus disassociate yourself from evil, or to inflict on me the severest penalty if you believe that the system and the law you are assisting to administer are good for the people of this country and that my activity is, therefore, injurious to the public weal."

Broomfield sentenced Gandhi to six years in jail, but observed that "no one would be better pleased than I if the government reduced the sentence." Gandhi was taken to Yeravda Central Jail in Poona.

Many observers noted that Gandhi seemed serene and even pleased at the course of events, and in the next two years in prison he read dozens of books, conducted a voluminous correspondence, and generally seemed to have remarshaled his strength.

Gandhi was released from jail in February 1924 after an operation for appendicitis. But he refrained from active political work, and instead spent the next few years thinking and writing about the religious and moral goals he envisioned, working at the Sabarmati *ashram*, and traveling the country preaching self-sufficiency for India. To this end he advocated cottage industries in the hundreds of thousands of villages of India, and especially the spinning of cloth. Only by providing work for themselves could Indians break the British yoke, he declared, and spinning was an essential means of doing this. The idea of a nation of millions of spinners was somewhat romantic if intended literally, but in a symbolic way it made perfect sense. Gandhi spent part of each day spinning and insisted that his *ashram* colleagues do the same, and it was taken up around the country. When he appeared in a

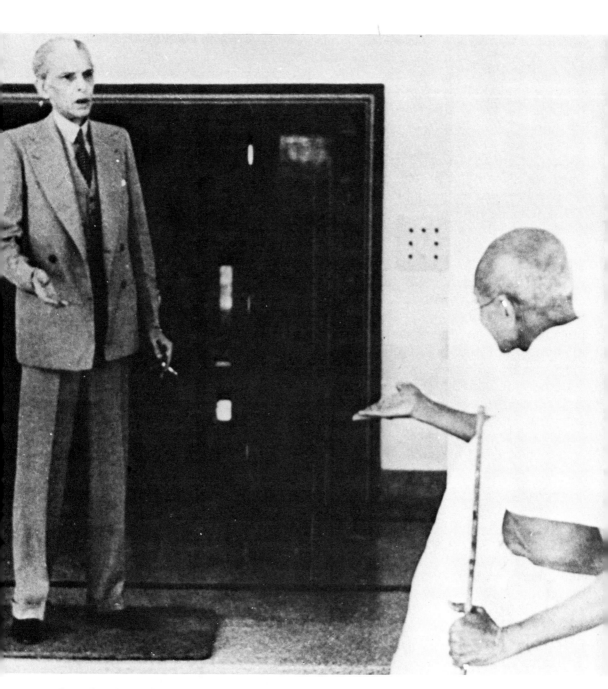

Moslem leader Mohammed Ali Jinnah (left) talking with Gandhi.

At right, Gandhi walks with Jawaharlal Nehru.

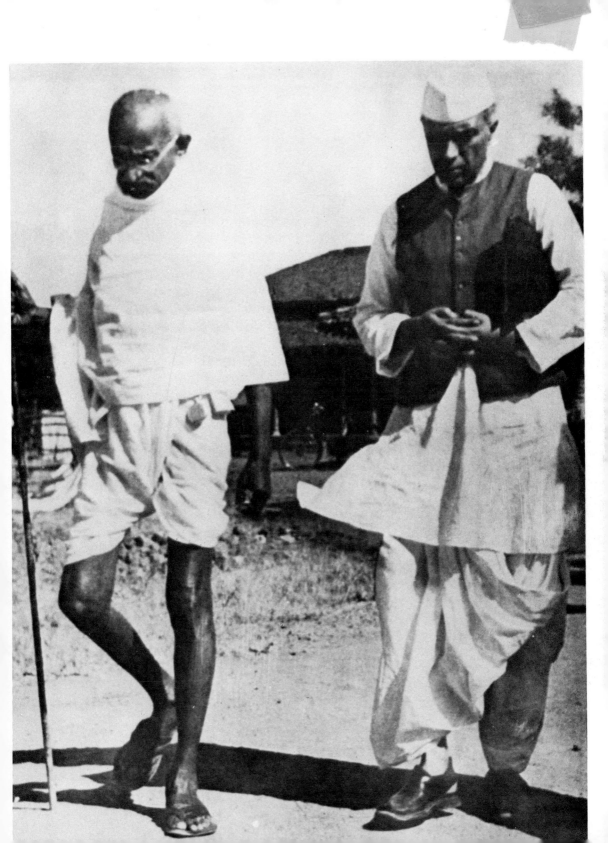

village, hundreds would turn out along his route squatting by their spinning wheels. Gandhi said the making of *khadi,* or homespun cloth, would be the symbol of Indians' fight for independence, and all over the country, and especially among politicians and Congress members, *khadi* became the accepted mode of dress.

All this was part of Gandhi's campaign for the purification of India, a process that, by adhering to the religious and moral standards he advocated, he felt would eventually overcome the British. Purification also meant friendship between Hindu and Moslem, a goal for which Gandhi worked ceaselessly but which seemed further than ever from accomplishment during these years, as new suspicions and inequities grew up. Sometimes the Hindu majority acted toward the Moslem minority as the British did toward Indians.

These were the years of consolidation, including in 1924 a twenty-one-day fast to purify himself.

Early in 1928 the machine started to move again. The immediate cause was the Simon Commission, a panel set up by the British (under a previous commitment known as the Montagu-Chelmsford reforms of 1919). The purpose of the commission was to review India's constitutional status. Gandhi and the leaders of the Congress party boycotted the commission, noting that there were no Indians on it and charging that in any case it was a charade because the government in London had no intention of granting home rule. There were demonstrations throughout India, which were often attacked by the police.

The Indians drew up their own proposed constitution for self-government, called the Nehru Report after Motilal Nehru, a Congress leader for many years and the father of Jawaharlal Nehru, later to be the first prime minister of independent India. There was dissension in the Indian ranks: Jawaharlal Nehru and the Bengali leader Subhas Chandra Bose opposed dominion status, calling instead for complete independence. At the Calcutta meeting of the Congress in December 1928 a compromise drafted by Gandhi was accepted. It stated that if Britain did not accept the Nehru Report within a year Congress would seek complete independence by nonviolent noncooperation.

By the time of the December 1929 Congress meeting in Lahore it was clear that the British were not about to grant anything. Jawaharlal Nehru, now officially Gandhi's heir, was elected president of the Congress. As 1930 opened Gandhi was searching for his next step. He declared January 26 Independence Day and soon after announced that he had decided on a new campaign of civil disobedience, with a specific goal—disobeying the salt-tax laws.

Salt

Like all the Mahatma's greatest victories, the Salt March was starkly simple in its conception. It was immediately understandable to all, however ignorant or unlettered, and supremely suitable for maximum media impact. The symbolism was crystal clear, the act itself uncomplicated but on a grand scale. The point could not be mistaken by followers, enemies, or the world at large. And like so many of Gandhi's campaigns, it had a wonderfully practical end as well.

Here was India, a country largely surrounded by salt water, yet its foreign rulers held the monopoly on making salt—and this in a land where the heat made salt a necessity of life. Every time an Indian bought salt he was paying a small but burdensome tax to his British rulers.

In accordance with his principles of *satyagraha*, Gandhi first wrote to the

I want world sympathy in this battle of Right against Might.

Gandhi M K Gandhi

5. 4. '30

British viceroy, Lord Irwin, declaring his intention to mount a massive campaign of civil disobedience. In his letter, dated March 2, 1930, he wrote what amounted to a statement of *satyagraha* principles.

"Dear Friend,

"Before embarking on civil disobedience and taking the risk I have dreaded to take all these years, I would fain approach you and find a way out. My personal faith is absolutely clear. I cannot intentionally hurt anything that lives, much less fellow human beings even though they may do the greatest wrong to me and mine. While, therefore, I hold British rule to be a curse, I do not intend to harm a single Englishman or any legitimate interest he may have in India.

"I must not be misunderstood. Though I hold British rule to be a curse, I do not, therefore, consider Englishmen in general to be worse than any other people on earth. I have the privilege of claiming many Englishmen as dearest friends. Indeed much that I have learned of the evil of British rule is due to the writings of frank and courageous Englishmen who have not hesitated to tell the unpalatable truth about that rule.

"In common with many of my countrymen, I had hugged the fond hope that the proposed Round Table Conference might furnish a solution [of Indian freedom]. But when you said plainly that you could not give any assurance that you or the British cabinet would pledge yourselves to support a scheme of full dominion status, the Round Table Conference could not possibly furnish the solution for which vocal India is consciously, and dumb millions unconsciously, thirsting.

"If India is to survive as a nation, if the slow death by starvation of her people is to stop, some remedy must be found for immediate relief. The proposed conference is certainly not the remedy. It is not a matter of carrying conviction by argument. The matter resolves itself into one of matching forces. Conviction or no conviction, Great Britain would defend her Indian commerce and interest by all the forces at her command. India must consequently evolve [nonviolent] force enough to free herself from that embrace of death.

"I know that in embarking on nonviolence I shall be running what might fairly be termed a mad risk, but the victories of truth have never been won without risks, often of the gravest character. Conversion of a nation that has consciously or unconsciously preyed upon another far more numerous, far more ancient, and no less cultured than itself is worth any amount of risk.

"I have deliberately used the word 'conversion.' For my ambition is no less than to convert the British people through nonviolence and thus make them see the wrong they have done to India. I do not seek to harm your people. I want to serve them even as I want to serve my own. I believe that I have always served them. I served them up to 1919 blindly. But when my eyes were opened, and I conceived of noncooperation, the object still was to

Gandhi on the Salt March. At right, Mrs. S. Naidu.

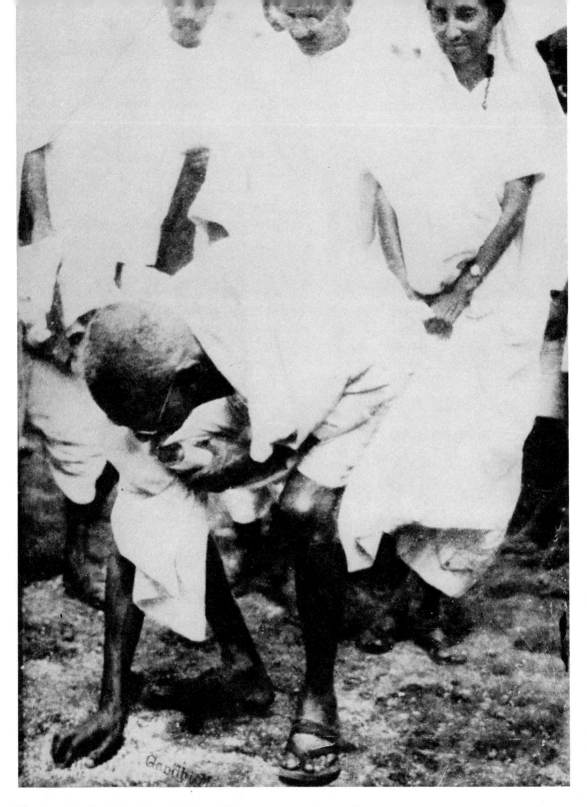

Gandhi picks up salt on the seashore at Dandi, April 5, 1930.

serve them. I employed the same weapon that I have in all humility successfully used against the dearest members of my family. If I have equal love for your people with mine, it will not long remain hidden. It will be acknowledged by them even as members of my family acknowledged it after they had tried me for several years. If people join me, as I expect they will, the sufferings they will undergo, unless the British nation retraces its steps first, will be enough to melt the stoniest hearts.

"This letter is not in any way intended as a threat but is a simple and sacred duty peremptory on a civil resister."

Thus with his usual mixture of philosophy, morality, and politics, and with his emphasis on "I" rather than "we," Gandhi set the stage for his most daring move.

A young Quaker friend of Gandhi's, Reginald Reynolds, delivered the letter personally to the viceroy's private secretary. The viceroy, through the secretary, wired a formal note in which he expressed regret "at Mr. Gandhi's contemplating a course of action which was clearly bound to involve the violation of the law and danger to public peace."

Gandhi's reply was to say: "I repudiate the law, and regard it as my sacred duty to break the mournful monotony of the compulsory peace that is choking the heart of the nation."

So Gandhi set about his plan. He would defy British law and Britain's economic interests.

He would make salt.

With a shrewd eye for maximum dramatic impact, he would march from the *ashram*—slowly, very slowly—to the sea, a distance of 241 miles, with a group of followers. No automobile, no train would be used, but on foot he and his people would march to the coastal town of Dandi, south of the *ashram*. There he would scoop salt water from the sea and make salt.

On March 12, 1930, the Mahatma, now sixty-one years old, and scores of *ashram* colleagues, as well as a contingent of the press corps, set out for Dandi. The residents of the town near the *ashram*, Ahmadabad, cheered the marchers on their way. Gandhi and his colleagues marched ten to fifteen miles a day, resting frequently, greeted by admirers and sympathizers and worshipers along the way. The viceroy, inclined to belittle the march, took no action, even as excitement over it grew with each day, especially as the newspaper correspondents reported the drama in detail and Indians along the route turned out to cheer and sometimes to join in the march.

Finally, on April 5, the party reached Dandi, and on the morning of the sixth they waded into the sea for a ritual bath and then, defying the law, Gandhi picked up salt from the seashore.

The march and the symbolic gesture gripped India's imagination. Suddenly everyone wanted to make salt, and the civil disobedience campaign spread throughout the country. Nehru wrote how he and his Congress colleagues produced some "unwholesome" salt, but noted that "it was really immaterial whether the stuff was good or bad; the main thing was to commit a breach of the obnoxious salt law, and we were successful in that, even though the quality of our salt was poor. As we saw the abounding enthusiasm of the people and the way salt-making was spreading like a prairie fire, we felt a little abashed and ashamed for having questioned the efficacy of this method when it was first proposed by Gandhiji. And we marveled at the amazing knack of the man to impress the multitude and make it act in an organized way."

Not unexpectedly, mass arrests soon began as the civil disobedience campaign grew, with thousands buying, selling, and making salt. The tiny bit of salt Gandhi had picked up was auctioned for a vast sum. Nehru was sentenced to six months in prison. The mayor of Calcutta, who publicly urged Indians not to wear foreign cloth, was jailed. The great Salt March fostered many salt marches by others, and on the seashore or by salty streams people broke the law—and newspapers around the world reported it day after day.

Ultimately, during the night of May 5, Gandhi was arrested, and the British went after any leader who had been involved.

By far the most moving, awful, and telling consequence of the *satyagraha* campaign was the "raid" to take over the government's Dharsana saltworks, north of Bombay, which Gandhi had planned before his arrest. A correspondent for United Press, Webb Miller, had been tipped off about the raid. Laden with a pack of sandwiches and two quart bottles of water, he set out on foot for the site from the nearest railroad station, about six miles away.

The demonstration was being led by Mrs. Sarojini Naidu, a poet and close associate of Gandhi. Some 2500 members of Congress and other Gandhi followers in *dhotis* and white caps were assembled on the blazingly hot plain. Facing them were 400 native policemen in khaki shorts and brown turbans, carrying five-foot clubs with steel tips. Inside the saltworks stockade were twenty-five riflemen. The images of that raid, in Miller's dramatic eyewitness account, have remained to this day the quintessential images of nonviolent civil disobedience, as wave after wave of unarmed men walked silently up to the club-wielding policemen and permitted themselves to be beaten senseless without raising an arm to protect themselves.

Miller reported:

"Those struck down fell sprawling, unconscious or writhing in pain with fractured skulls or broken shoulders. In two or three minutes the ground was quilted with bodies. Great patches of blood widened on their white clothes. When every one of the first column had been knocked down, stretcher-bearers rushed up unmolested by the police and carried off the injured to a thatched hut which had been arranged as a temporary hospital.

"Then another column formed. Although everyone knew that within a few minutes he would be beaten down,

Gandhi, center, on the famous Salt March.

perhaps killed, I could detect no signs of wavering or fear. There was no fight, no struggle; the marchers simply walked forward until struck down."

At one point, the demonstrators sat on the ground near the salt pans in groups of twenty-five and made no effort to get closer. They were similarly beaten bloody as they sat there, without making any attempt to ward off the blows.

Miller continued:

"In the middle of the morning V. J. Patel arrived. He had been leading the *swaraj* (self-rule) movement since Gandhi's arrest, and had just resigned as president of the Indian Legislative Assembly in protest against the British. Scores surrounded him, knelt, and kissed his feet. Sitting on the ground under a mango tree, Patel said: 'All hope of reconciling India with the British empire is lost forever. I can understand any government's taking people into custody and punishing them for breaches of the law, but I cannot understand how any government that calls itself civilized could deal as savagely and brutally with nonviolent, unresisting men as the British have this morning.' "

Tagore explained the real result of the bloody *satyagraha* campaign: "Europe has completely lost her former moral prestige in Asia. She is no longer regarded as the champion throughout the world of fair dealing and the exponent of high principle, but as the upholder of western race supremacy and the exploiter of those outside her own borders."

The Mahatma in London

Group photo taken in Marseilles en route to London, 1931.
From left: C. F. Andrews, Gandhi, Muriel Lester, Mahadev Desai,
Mirabehn, Pyarelal and an English friend.

Britain's embarrassment over the Salt March was matched only by the continuing civil disobedience throughout India. A Round Table conference was held in London in November 1930 to debate the Indian problem, but no Congress members were invited. There was a possibility that a second conference would welcome Congress, but most of its leaders were in jail. This reference to the possibility of another meeting seemed to be a broad hint by London to the Viceroy in India, Lord Irwin (later to be Lord Halifax), that he ought to be doing something, so he freed Gandhi and a couple of dozen other leaders.

Irwin and Gandhi set up a series of meetings that was to result in what became known as the Gandhi-Irwin Pact or the Delhi Pact. The first meeting was held on February 17, 1931. It took an archimperialist, Winston Churchill, to see the true political meaning of that meeting. Although his remarks are remembered mostly for his vivid and insulting description of Gandhi, the thrust of what he had to say showed a shrewd sense of what was happening. He spoke of the "alarming and also nauseating and humiliating spectacle of this onetime Inner Temple lawyer, now seditious fakir, striding half-naked up the steps of the viceroy's palace, there to negotiate and parley on equal terms." Churchill may have underestimated Gandhi, but he saw clearly that a new turn had been reached in which Indians weren't begging or pleading for their cause, but negotiating on equal footing.

After twenty-four hours of talks spread over eight meetings, Gandhi and Irwin agreed on a pact that called for release of most prisoners, allowing a limited amount of making salt, and the end of the civil disobedience campaign. Gandhi was criticized for what many saw as a sellout, but he maintained as he had in earlier and similar situations that a *satyagrahi* has to trust his opponent and that every means must be taken to seek peaceful solutions. The pact, in fact, did not accomplish very much for India, beyond its symbolic value in being the result of a negotiation, but it led to one of those media events by which the world came to know Gandhi so well.

From September 12 to December 5, 1931, Gandhi attended a second Round Table Conference in London, accompanied by a number of close aides; he was the only official Congress representative. Those accompanying him included Mirabehn, an Englishwoman whose real name was Madeleine Slade. She had joined Gandhi in 1924 and was welcomed to the *ashram* as a daughter. Mirabehn—the name given her by Gandhi—was the daughter of an English admiral, but her life had been a search for some direction, some cause. She had tried Beethoven but found she had no talent for music; through the French biographer of Beethoven and Gandhi, Romain Rolland, she had learned about Gandhi and decided to devote her life to his cause.

Others with Gandhi included his youngest son, Devadas; Mahadev Desai, his longtime secretary and confidant, whose detailed diaries have ever since been a gold mine for biographers of Gandhi; Pyarelal Nayyar; G. D. Birla, a textile magnate; Pandit Malaviya; and Mrs. Naidu, who had led the Salt March.

Gandhi provided London with a three-ring circus. Newsmen and ordinary Londoners followed him wherever he went, and the papers and newsreels were full of the beguiling figure in his white *dhoti* as he walked the streets of London and other English cities, met common people and dignitaries, joked with children, and in no time made himself a beloved visitor.

Gandhi's colorful and controversial fame had preceded him, for he had traveled steerage from India, accompanied not only by his aides but also by a couple of goats, as he drank only goat's milk. The little brown man in the loincloth and shawl took London by storm, and only added to the Mahatma cult that had grown up in the West.

Accommodations had been arranged for him by Charles Andrews and Henry Polak, and he stayed in a poor neighborhood at the Kingsley Hall Settlement, although for convenience he also had an office in Knightsbridge. He broadcast to America (blithely saying into an open microphone, "Do I

A session of the Second Round Table Conference, in London in 1931.

93

Dr. Hewlett Johnson, Dean of Canterbury, and Mirabehn
with Gandhi in England.

At left, Gandhi at 10 Downing Street after meeting
with British Prime Minister MacDonald.

talk into this thing?''), met Prime Minister Ramsay MacDonald, and renewed his friendship with Henry Salt. He made little jokes that the press ate up (talking about the plus-four trousers then popular among men, he remarked, "I wear minus-fours"), visited people in their homes, and always had time for children, who followed him in the streets, shouting "Gandhi, where's your trousers?"

Visiting cloth-mill workers who had been out of work because of the antiforeign-cloth drives he had mounted, he heard them say that in his place they would have done the same.

He met George Bernard Shaw, a fellow vegetarian, who modestly referred to himself as Mahatma Minor when they met and who later, when asked what he thought about the meeting, said, "You might as well ask for someone's impression of the Himalayas."

He met Charlie Chaplin but had never seen any of his movies, so the meeting was less than a roaring success.

There was no question that his public releations sense endeared him to the British public, but the conference itself, held at St. James's Palace, got nowhere. Perhaps Gandhi was not at his best: he sometimes

A crowd of Londoners try to see Gandhi.

Charlie Chaplin sits at left of Gandhi.   Mrs. Naidu stands at right. Others are unidentified.

Gandhi arrives at a Lancashire cotton mill to speak
with the workers.

Gandhi plants a tree outside Kingsley Hall in London in remembrance of his stay there.

attended meetings on only two hours' sleep.

Before he left England he visited King George V and Queen Mary wearing his usual *dhoti*. Asked if he felt he should have worn something more, he replied that the king wore enough for both of them.

On December 5 he left England, never to see it again. Mirabehn persuaded him to stop in Switzerland to see Rolland, and they visited for three days. Rolland described Gandhi at this time:

"The little man, bespectacled and toothless, was wrapped in white burnoose, but his legs, thin as heron's stilts, were bare. His shaven head, with its few coarse hairs, was uncovered and wet with rain. He came to me with a dry laugh, his mouth open like a good dog panting, and flung an arm around me.''

Rolland played some Beethoven for Gandhi, but the Mahatma's musical knowledge and tastes remained strictly Hindu, except for some Christian hymns.

Gandhi and his party then stopped in Rome for an audience with the pope, but the Vatican barred the visit because of his sparse attire. Gandhi did meet Mussolini, whom he later described as looking like a butcher.

Gandhi, right, with Romain Rolland, whom he visited in Switzerland on his way back to India.

A Fast and Prison

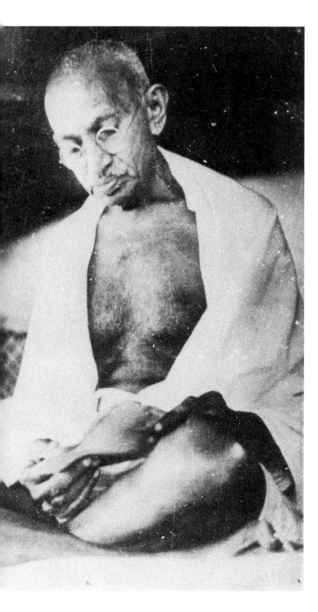

Despite the failure of the conference in London, Gandhi arrived home in Bombay on December 28 to be greeted as a hero. To the British he remained a dangerous enemy, however. Civil disobedience and government repression continued, and plans were already underway to arrest him as soon as a pretext could be found. On January 4, 1932, he was arrested in Bombay under the government's emergency regulations, and was sent to Yeravda once more. There was no trial, no hearing. The new viceroy, Lord Willingdon, had simply ordered the arrest.

Along with Gandhi, all of Congress's leaders were rounded up and put in jail, and Congress itself was declared outlawed—although it continued to function surreptitiously. Civil disobedience broke out again on a large scale, with renewed cloth boycotts, tax strikes, and salt-tax defiance. During January and February more than 32,000 people were convicted of political offenses. Even Mirabehn, still technically an English subject, was imprisoned for three months. Under severe repression measures and without Gandhi and other leaders on hand to marshal Indian forces, the furor died down.

While in prison Gandhi actively kept up with affairs, and was especially

incensed when in March the
government announced it had a new
plan for dividing the country into
electorates on the basis of religion.
Hindus, Moslems, Sikhs, Europeans,
and so on, would each be considered a
separate entity—part of the empire's
long-standing desire to keep the
country divided and weak. The plan
also called for a separate electorate for
Untouchables—something the
Untouchables themselves had been
calling for but which Gandhi saw only
as another nail in the coffin of Indian
unity.

Therefore, on September 20, Gandhi
announced he would fast unto death
unless the Untouchables plan was
rescinded. His threat was directed, of
course, as much or more at Indians as
at the British, for he continued to
regard untouchability as a blight on
the Indian subcontinent and as a major
force against Indian progress. The
effect was unprecedented. Moslem and
Untouchable leaders rallied to him.
The keepers of Hindu temples opened
them to Untouchables. Hindus of other
castes sat down and broke bread
publicly with Untouchables, whom
Gandhi had dubbed Harijans—children
of God. Untouchables and other
castes reached compromises on
representation.

Nehru's memoir on the events
captures the sense of wonder at the
ability of Gandhi to marshal the people
of India. Nehru, using the affectionate
term Bapu—"father," extended later to

Gandhi with Mirabehn.

mean "father of the nation"—said of Gandhi:

"I felt angry with him at his religious and sentimental approach to a political question and his frequent references to God in connection with it. If Bapu died! What would India be like then? And then a strange thing happened to me. I had quite an emotional crisis, and at the end of it I felt calmer, and the future seemed not so dark. Bapu had a curious knack of doing the right thing at the psychological moment. Then came news of the tremendous upheaval all over the country, a magic wave of enthusiasm running through Hindu society, and untouchability appeared to be doomed. What a magician, I thought, was this little man sitting in Yeravda prison, and how well he knew how to pull the strings that move people's hearts!"

Agreement was reached among Indians on September 26, and later that day the British agreed to what became known as the Yeravda Pact, under which the idea of a separate electorate was dropped. Gandhi had been growing weaker as the fast progressed, and when the British acceptance was announced he broke his fast with a sip of orange juice. The country rejoiced, although Gandhi reminded everyone that he would fast again if untouchability reform was not actively pursued within a reasonable time.

The Untouchables campaign prompted Gandhi to another action— publication of a newspaper dealing with the problem. He called it *Harijan* and, from prison, directed its

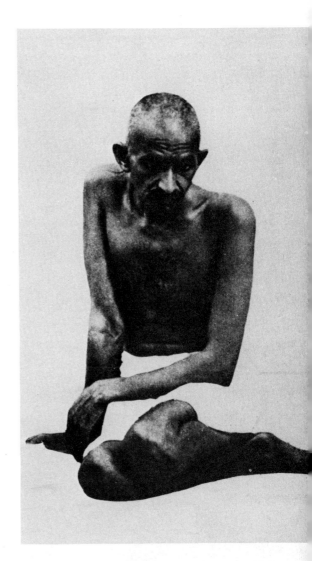

publication in Poona, financed by the textile manufacturer Birla. The first issue was published in February 1933, and the subject was one about which Gandhi continued to brood.

Then, not for the first time, Gandhi heard a voice that told him what to do next. On the night of April 23, 1933, he wrote, "some voice—within or without, I cannot say—whispers, 'Thou must go on a fast.' 'How many days?' I

Central Prison at Yeravda, where Gandhi was interned.

ask. The voice again says, 'Twenty-one days.' " The next morning he announced he would start a twenty-one-day fast on May 8, while still in prison. The purpose, he said, was "heart prayer for purification of myself and my associates for greater vigilance and watchfulness in connection with the *Harijan* cause." His friends and his doctors feared he could not survive, but he insisted. The government, not wanting to have him die in prison, released him. He went to a friend's house where he continued the fast, breaking it with a glass of orange juice on May 29.

In July he announced that he was giving up Sabarmati *ashram*, although it continued to serve as a Gandhian center. He decided another demonstration for Indian independence was needed, and he mounted a march

Gandhi eats a last meal before beginning a fast at Rajkot.

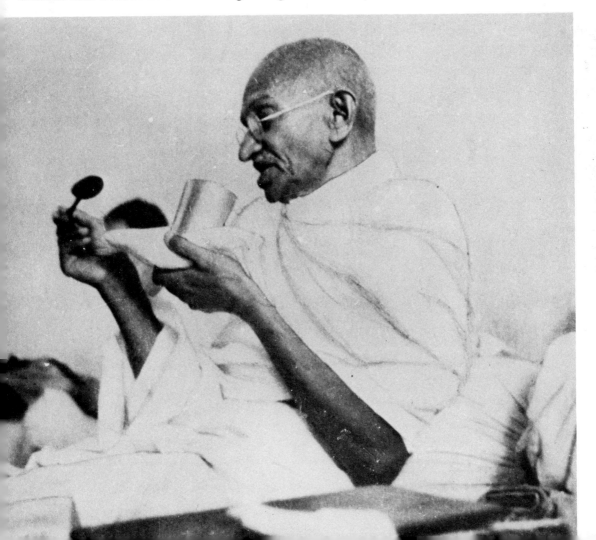

Gandhi on a morning walk.

of several dozen companions and himself to court arrest. Before the march could start he and his followers were arrested—it was August 1, 1933— and he was sent to jail for a year. This time there was a brief trial during which he gave his occupation as "spinner, weaver, and farmer" and his permanent address as Yeravda jail. He demanded to be allowed to work for the Untouchables while in prison, but the authorities demurred, and he began

yet another fast to the death. The alarmed officials transferred him to a hospital, then released him, and he ended his fast. It was far from being his last fast.

In the fall of 1933 he toured India again, this time on behalf of the Untouchables, proclaiming that only by lifting the curse could India realize its ambitions for independence. By then the entire civil disobedience movement had waned, and Gandhi had left the center stage of politics. He even alienated many supporters in January 1934 when, after an earthquake in Bihar took thousands of lives, he declared it was a divine judgment on untouchability.

In April 1934 he called an official halt to the *satyagraha* campaign and in October resigned from Congress, although continuing to be consulted by its leaders. Despite his receding into the background, it was clear that Gandhi had had a profound effect. Britain was gradually, if reluctantly, moving toward the day when there would be independence or something like it, and it was coming in large part because, as Gandhi had predicted, his truth force had forced the British to see that theirs was a hopeless cause.

Gandhi had set up a new *ashram* headquarters near Wardha, called Sevagram ("service village"), where some years before he had set up a sister *ashram* to Sabarmati but had not used it as a headquarters. One of his visitors there was the renowned American birth control advocate Margaret Sanger, who thought she had in Gandhi a sympathetic hearer. But it became clear that where she saw pleasure in sexual union and saw contraception as the means to birth control, Gandhi saw celibacy as the solution to population problems and sexual union as something to be performed only the few times in life one wanted children. Mrs. Sanger reported: "After reading his autobiography, I thought I saw the cause of his inhibitions. He himself had had the feeling which he termed lust, and now he hated it. It formed an emotional pivot in his brain around which centered everything having to do with sex."

Gandhi with his secretary Pyarelal's niece.

"Quit India"

Britain had been preparing a constitution for India. It was officially promulgated in August 1934 and put into effect in 1937. It called for self-rule for India in stages. Nehru opposed it, calling it a "charter of slavery," and called for noncooperation. Another faction of Congress approved of it, however. A key element in the constitution was the transfer of most government powers to elected provincial governments. Congress finally accepted the plan, fearing that if it stayed aloof the Moslem League would gain control.

But all these moves were dwarfed, even in India, by the coming of World War II. Gandhi's long-held views on how to deal with an opponent came to the fore again. Some Congress leaders demanded that Indians use the opportunity, now that Britain's back was against the wall, to press for

Gandhi, left, with Maulana Azad.

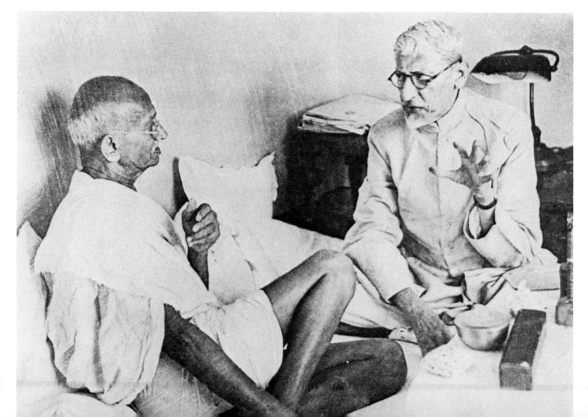

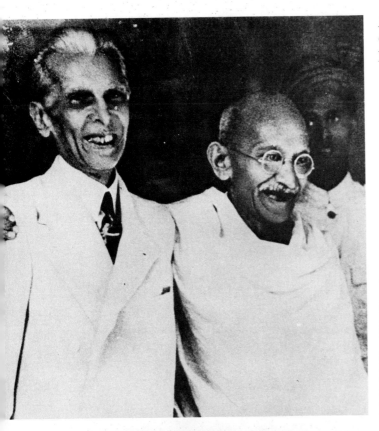

Mohammed Ali Jinnah with
Gandhi during their talks in
Bombay, 1944.

Below, Gandhi arrives at a
prayer meeting in Delhi in
1945. The men with him,
from left, are Acharya
Kripalani, Khan Abdul
Ghaffar Khan, and Jawaharlal
Nehru.

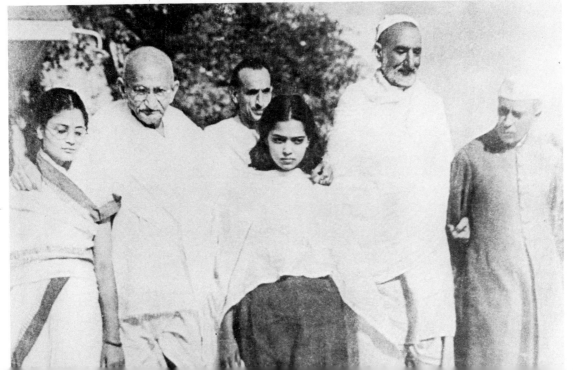

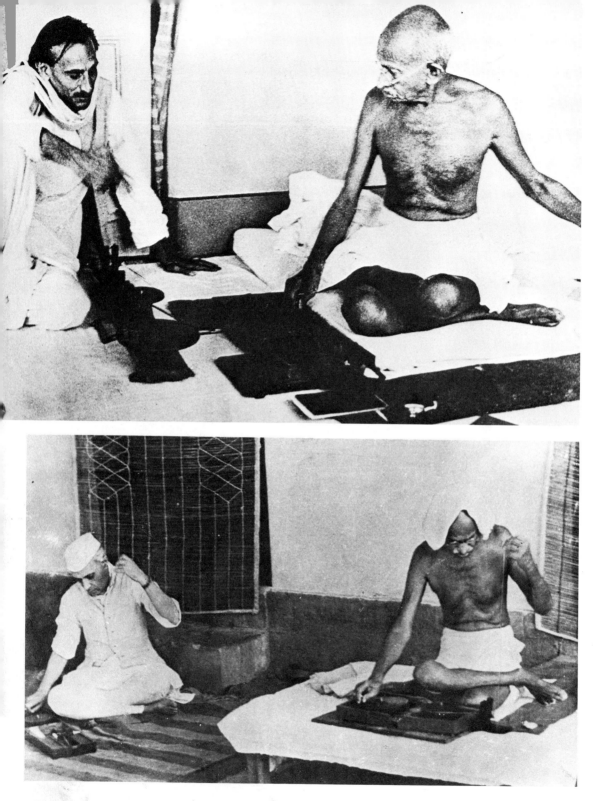

Above left, Gandhi with Acharya Kripalani. Below left, spinning with Nehru.

independence now; to tell Britain that India would fight on Britain's side only as a free and independent nation. Gandhi, however, refused to stab Britain in the back in its hour of desperation and suggested instead a compromise whereby individual acts of *satyagraha* would be mounted, avoiding the large-scale disruption of a mass *satyagraha,* and thereby avoiding harm to the British war effort.

Gandhi chose Vinoba Bhave, whom he regarded as the perfect *satyagrahi.* Bhave would be sent around the country speaking out against the horrors of war, thereby courting arrest, but not interfering with the country's ability to support the British war effort. In October 1940 Bhave crisscrossed villages near Wardha, making antiwar speeches. After three days he was arrested and sentenced to three months in prison.

Gandhi's ambivalence, reflected in this low-key *satyagraha,* was also seen

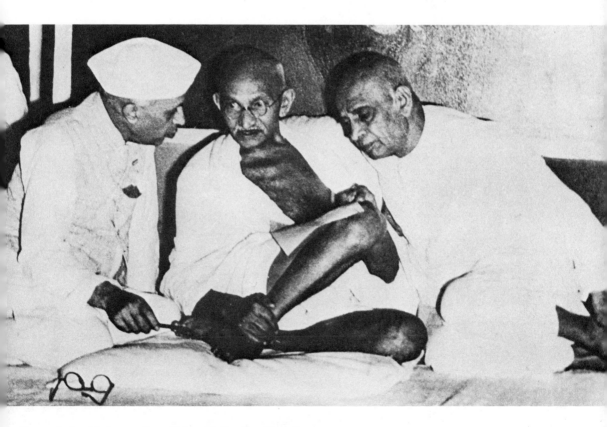

From left, Nehru, Gandhi and Sardar Patel.

in Gandhi's attempts to reason by letter with Hitler. For Gandhi the war was a distant problem, not directly involving India. He believed that nonviolent noncooperation could melt even the heart of a Hitler. Even Kallenbach, as stalwart a Gandhian as existed, had to draw the line at such a view. Gandhi wrote to Hitler twice, getting no reply.

Small-scale *satyagraha* continued, and Gandhi's next choice as *satyagraha*, Jawaharlal Nehru, was also arrested and was sentenced to four years in jail. This particularly angered Indians, and more protest meetings took place. A third aide, Patel, was also arrested, and so it went, until more than 20,000 Congress supporters were in jail.

The political situation created by this campaign had some unforeseen consequences. For one thing, it divided the Congress, with Bose demanding total rebellion while Gandhi continued to press for nonviolent noncooperation. Perhaps even more important, with so many Congress leaders in jail,

Gandhi, followed by Mahadev Desai, leaves the Calcutta Presidency Jail after interviewing political prisoners.

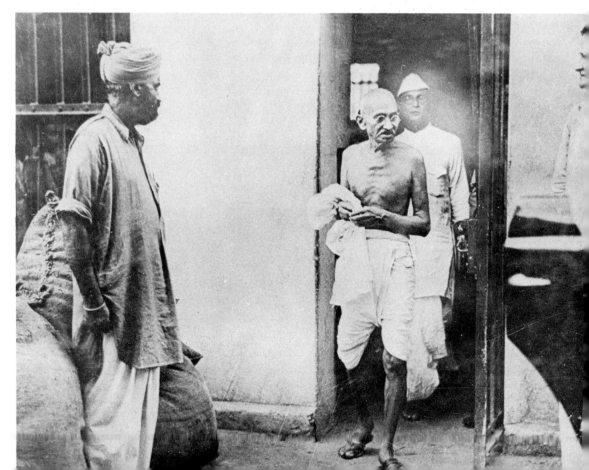

Moslems moved into positions of power left vacant by Hindus.

In 1941, just before the Japanese attack on Pearl Harbor, Churchill, expecting Japanese participation in the war, ordered all the leading Congress prisoners released. He sent Sir Stafford Cripps, a left-wing member of parliament, to try for another constitutional plan that Gandhi and Congress would accept, but the plan, while granting India the right to self-government after the war, and even the right to secede from the commonwealth, also would allow any princely state, province, or religious group to work out a separate deal with Britain. Gandhi saw this only as portending not one India, but a number of Indias, a prospect that horrified him, for he had always maintained that independence should come to a united India. "My firm opinion," Gandhi said, "is that the British should leave India now in an orderly manner."

He drew up a plan, which Mirabehn delivered personally to Nehru, that called for an orderly British withdrawal immediately. This came to be known as the "Quit India" resolution, although Gandhi did not coin that phrase. It was directed at the British government, not at the British army, which would be permitted to remain. There were fears that if the British did leave at once the state might fall apart. "Leave India to God," Gandhi had said. "If that is too much, then leave her to anarchy."

As Congress debated the import of the Quit India move, Gandhi refrained from actually calling for open rebellion. Speaking to a Congress committee, he said: "Here is a *mantra*, a short one, that I give you. You may imprint it on your hearts and let every breath of yours give expression to it. The *mantra* is 'Do or Die.' We shall either free India or die in the attempt."

But nothing happened. The British bided their time. On August 8, 1942, Congress passed the Quit India resolution, and on August 9 Gandhi, Desai, Mirabehn, and other Congress leaders were arrested. These three were taken for imprisonment to the palace of the Aga Khan near Poona, a site that had been carefully chosen as a comfortable prison for the Mahatma and his friends. With Gandhi and the leaders in jail, the *satyagraha* campaign quickly erupted into mass violence around the country, despite Gandhi's exhortation before he went to jail that a *hartal* should be nonviolent. Things were out of his control now.

Four days after the arrests Desai died in jail, at age 50. Kasturba, who had been arrested the day after Gandhi and had joined him in the palace imprisonment, especially bemoaned Desai's death, as he was one of her closest friends in Gandhi's entourage.

Outside the jail violence went on unchecked, some of it engendered by Congress left-wingers, and there were hundreds of deaths. Railroad tracks were torn up and stations and post offices—symbols of British rule—were set ablaze. The viceroy, Lord Linlithgow, blamed Gandhi for the violence. Gandhi sent out a stream of letters protesting that the violence had been touched off by the jailings of

Kasturba washes her husband's feet.

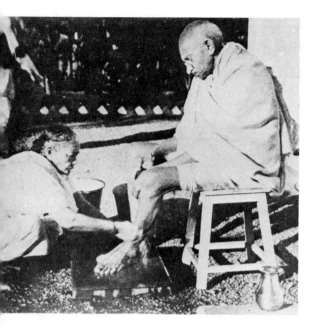

himself and his colleagues, but the viceroy refused to back down. As a result, in February 1943, while still in his palace prison, Gandhi undertook yet another twenty-one-day fast to clear up the "misunderstanding." The viceroy pointed out that Gandhi was breaking his own rules about fasting only to prod the consciences of friends, not to coerce opponents. Fears mounted that Gandhi might not survive, and government doctors were always in attendance. The fast ended as scheduled, and Gandhi survived, but his health had deteriorated permanently, and nothing had been accomplished.

The months in jail dragged on. Gandhi tried once more to give

Front row, from left: Nehru, Gandhi, Mahadev Desai and Dr. Pattabhi Sitaramayya walk to a Working Committee meeting at Wardha in 1940.

Kasturba

Right: Gandhi and friends leave Kasturba's funeral.

Kasturba lessons in reading, writing, and geography, but it was too late for Bapu to teach Ba ("Mother") anything. Time was running out. On February 22, 1944, Kasturba died from complications of heart palpitations and bronchitis. Gandhi refused to allow the use of penicillin, out of religious conviction and because of the feeling that in any case it was too late to save her. Gandhi held her in his arms as she died. A funeral attended by about 150 people was held on the palace grounds. "I cannot imagine life without Ba," Gandhi said. "Her passing has left a vacuum which will never be filled. We were a couple outside the ordinary."

As a result of public pressure and doctors' advice (Gandhi had suffered a malaria attack, hookworm, and amoebic dysentery following his fast), the government released Gandhi on May 6, 1944. It was the last time he would be in prison.

As soon as Gandhi was free he resumed his Congress activities, particularly seeking some kind of understanding with Mohammed Ali Jinnah, whose Moslem League had made great inroads while Congress

Nehru and Gandhi at All India Congress, August 8, 1942.

At the August 8 Congress meeting that adopted the "Quit India" resolution.

leaders were in jail. Jinnah was looking forward to a separate Moslem country, to be known as Pakistan, as part of an independence agreement with Britain— a goal long sought by the divide-and-conquer mentality of the British. Gandhi had by this time conceded that perhaps some sort of Moslem Pakistan would be necessary. But Jinnah wanted division before or coincidental with independence. Gandhi looked ahead to some later arrangement. They could not agree.

In June 1945 the viceroy called a meeting of Congress and Moslem leaders in Simla. Gandhi had retreated from Congress politics again, and attended only as an individual. Jinnah declared that the Moslems, representing a quarter of the population, should have political parity with the Hindus. Congress, in its turn, saw the British as inevitably committed to favoring the Moslems.

To figure out how power should be transferred to the Indians, Britain's Prime Minister Clement Attlee sent a mission to India in March 1946. The mission recommended a three-part India: a central union for defense and

A crowd being teargassed by police after passage of the "Quit India" resolution.

Aga Khan Palace in Poona, where Gandhi was interned from August 1942 to May 1944.

Gandhi spinning in Bombay, 1945.

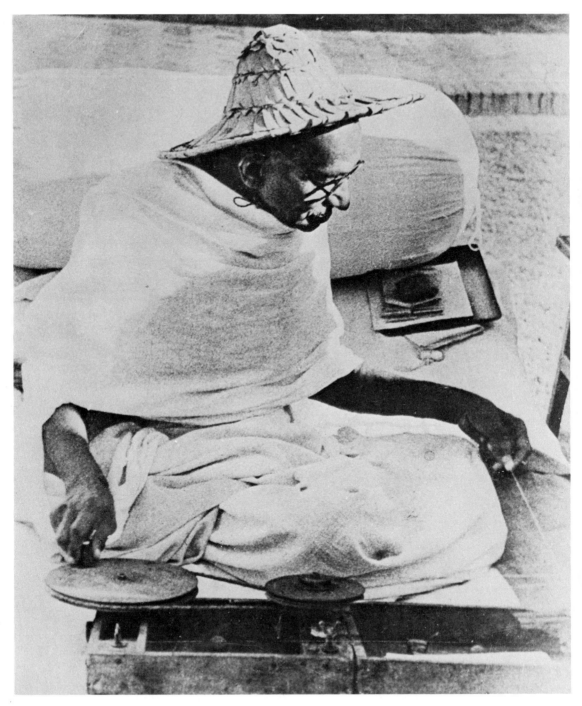

Spinning at Birla House, New Delhi.

foreign affairs; semiautonomous regional groups of provinces and states (one largely Hindu, one Moslem, and one balanced between the two), and individual provinces and states for local matters. Gandhi at first was inclined to dismiss the plan, then more or less accepted it.

In April, however, the Moslem League vowed to achieve a separate Pakistan by force if necessary. Jinnah declared: "We will fight for it, and if necessary we will die for it; but take it we must—or perish." The Moslems were actually divided over whether there should be a separate Pakistan, but communal fears were real, and political pressures—fostered over the years by the British—gave the declaration great power. In August, therefore, Jinnah called for "direct action" to achieve a separate Pakistan. He never publicly spelled out what he meant, but the populace made its own

Attending to his correspondence.

decision. He declared August 16 Direct Action Day, and that morning Moslem gangs in Calcutta opened what later would be known as the "great killings." For four days the mayhem continued, until more than five thousand Hindu lives had been sacrificed to the Moslem cause. The Hindus, of course, retaliated, and the religious and communal bloodshed mounted on a huge scale.

The violence continued to spread throughout eastern Bengal, with reports of mass killings in Chittagong and Noakhali—murder, arson, rape, and religious atrocities—as Hindus were forced to profess Moslem commandments. The massacres in Noakhali began on October 10 and went on for a week, but not until October 20 did news of the situation reach the outside world, as fleeing survivors told what had happened. (The Indian press had long since been silenced by the British.) It was civil war. Gandhi, horrified, declared in Delhi that he would go to Noakhali and die if necessary to stop the killing.

He stopped first in Calcutta, and on November 6 set out for Noakhali. In village after village he saw burned bodies of Hindus, heard stories of forced conversions, of kidnappings and looting.

He tramped barefoot through mud and swamps preaching nonviolence.

Gandhi on his way to meet the British Viceroy at Simla.

128

Gandhi with a British Parliamentary delegation, 1946.

Sardar Patel (left) and Manibehn with Gandhi in Simla.

Gandhi with Lord
and Lady
Mountbatten. Lord
Louis was the last
Viceroy in India.

Gandhi at the Lahore Railway Station while on his way to Kashmir in July 1947.

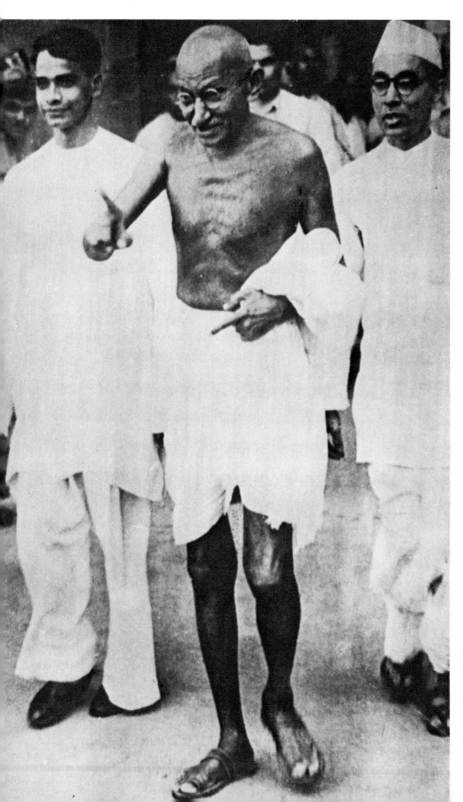

Gandhi jokes with
journalists, 1946.
At right, the Red
Fort, Delhi, on
India's
Independence Day,
August 15, 1947.

His aides would drop off at each Moslem village they passed through to protect the villagers, and Gandhi set up a headquarters in Srirampur, where he stayed through December. Then, when Hindu massacres of Moslems broke out in Bihar, he went through a similar pilgrimage there, toward the end of February 1947. Meanwhile, a new viceroy, Lord Mountbatten, had arrived in Delhi, and Gandhi went there to meet him.

Gandhi once more proposed a single India, but in a daring move suggested that Jinnah and a Moslem government should rule it. Nehru and Congress opposed the idea and Gandhi gave in, feeling he was a failure.

On August 15, 1947, the official declaration of Indian independence

Indians celebrate Independence at the Red Fort. Gandhi was in Calcutta fasting and working for peace between Hindus and Moslems.

Gandhi crosses a bamboo bridge in an East Bengal village where fighting was going on over partition.

took place, with the country divided into Pakistan on the east and west of India. Gandhi was in Calcutta on the fateful day, still traveling and preaching peace.

Gandhi had asked Shaheed Suhrawardy, a Moslem League leader who was believed to have been responsible for the Direct Action campaign, if he would agree to live under the same roof with him while he sought to bring peace to the area. Suhrawardy, who had previously asked Gandhi to stay in the area to continue his work for peace, agreed, even though both men realized they would be the targets of violence and might be killed. They had chosen a house called Haidari Mansion, owned by a Moslem woman, but in the Hindu section of Calcutta.

The house was surrounded by mobs, some seeking *darshan*, others angrily threatening Gandhi. One small group of Hindu youths got in to see Gandhi and asked why he had come to Calcutta when the Moslems were in danger, but was not there when Hindus were threatened. Gandhi said only that he had come to bring peace, and after some more talk, it was clear he had worked his will on them and they were won over.

On the day before Independence Day, Suhrawardy addressed the crowd from the house, and when someone asked whether he had been responsible for August's massacre he admitted responsibility. The admission cleared the air and a feeling of relief and calm swept the crowd. Almost simultaneously there were reports of

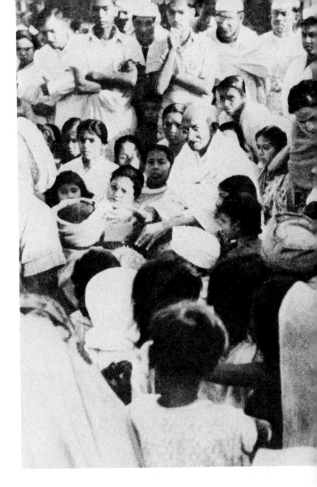

At a prayer meeting in a disturbed village.

Hindus and Moslems marching arm in arm through the city. On Independence Day there was peace and brotherhood in the city. It was not to last.

Communal war continued throughout the country as Hindus and Sikhs fled from Pakistan and Moslems fled from India in the greatest cross-migration in history. Altogether, 12 million people fled in one direction or another, and within a year half a million people had died. The world had rarely seen the like.

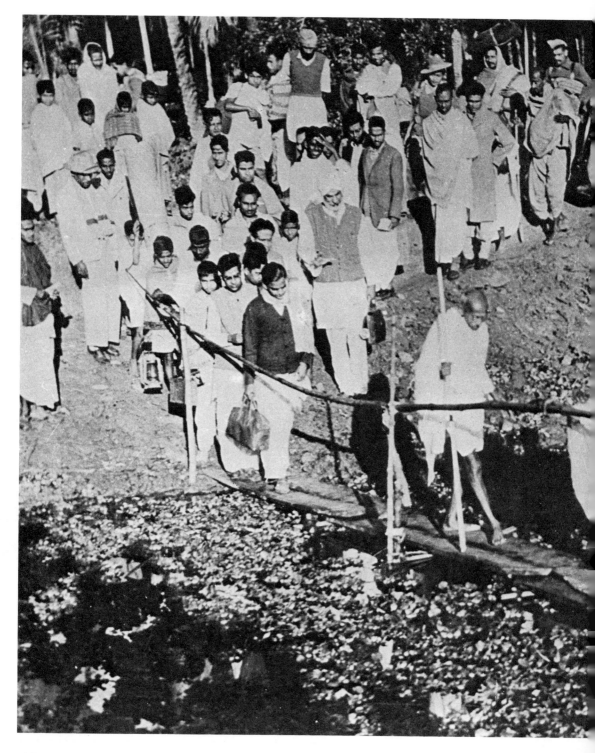

140

Gandhi visits a ravaged Moslem village after riots in Bihar in 1947.

141

Entering a ruined Moslem building in Bihar.

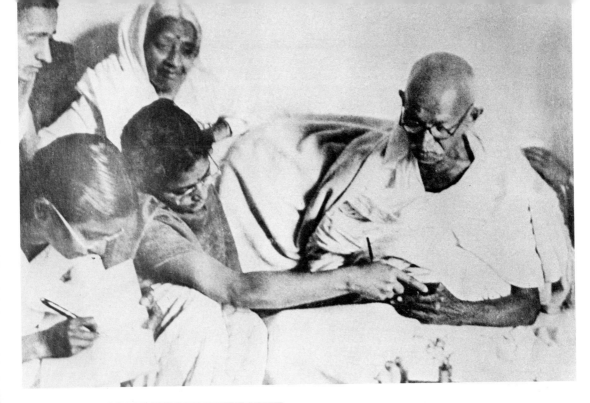

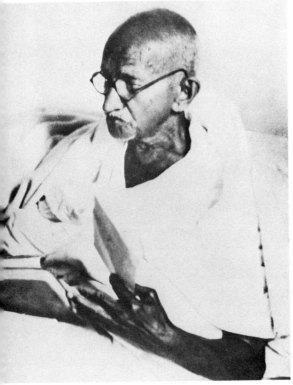

Gandhi on the final day of his last fast at Birla House, New Delhi, January 18, 1948.

On September 1 Gandhi began another fast "to the death" as renewed violence broke out in Calcutta. This time it took four days before the mobs calmed down enough for Gandhi to be told that his fast had worked, that Hindus felt they would be guilty of having caused his death and Moslems feared they would be massacred if he died.

As 1948 dawned Gandhi was in Delhi, living at Birla House. Although violence had died down somewhat, even Delhi was the scene of repeated atrocities as Hindu mobs gradually

pushed out the remaining Moslems. On January 13 Gandhi undertook another fast in behalf of communal unity. This fast ended in five days, as the violence wound down.

On January 30 Gandhi started the day with a walk in the garden and ate breakfast about 9:30, then rested. He received visitors, including *Life* photographer Margaret Bourke-White, whose portraits of Gandhi had done much to fix his image in the western mind. At 5:00 p.m. he walked into the garden again for a large prayer meeting, the first since his fast had ended. Among those on the lawn was Nathuram Vinayak Godse, publisher of a weekly in Poona. He was part of a conspiracy among orthodox Hindus who wanted Gandhi assassinated, believing that his work for religious toleration had caused the loss of a united Hindu India and had resulted in the creation of Pakistan.

Godse, as he said later, "firmly believed that the teachings of absolute *ahimsa* would ultimately result in the emasculation of the Hindu community."

Godse watched as Gandhi approached the crowd. The Mahatma leaned for support, as was his custom, on the shoulders of two young women. Godse came up to Gandhi, bowed, then pulled out a revolver and fired three shots. Gandhi died instantly.

Birla House. To the right is the room where Gandhi spent his last days.

One of the last photos taken of Gandhi.
He walks to prayers at Birla House, January 29, 1948.

After the first shock, the horrified crowd demanded *darshan*, so Gandhi's body was taken to the roof of Birla House and illuminated with a searchlight.

The next day, with Gandhi's body on a gun carriage, the funeral procession wound through Delhi for five hours, with millions of people watching the cortege until it reached the sacred Yamuna River, where the body was placed on a raft and cremated.

A final image, from Gandhi's autobiography, the image of the seeker he always was: "To see the universal and all-pervading Spirit of Truth face to face one must be able to love the meanest of creatures as oneself."

At right, a view of Gandhi's funeral procession in Del
on January 31, 194

The funeral procession in Delhi.

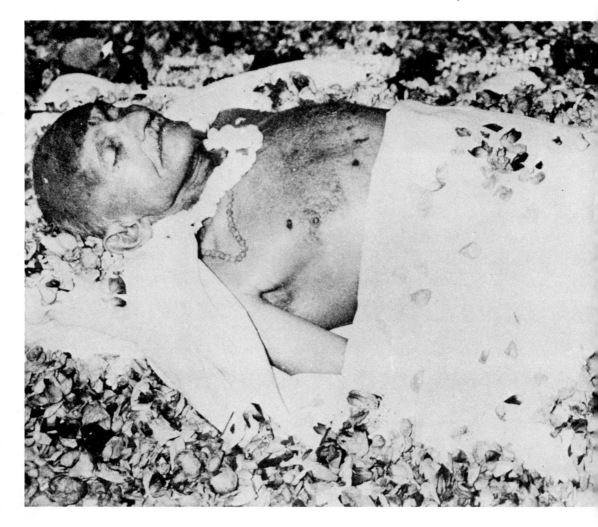

Gandhi's body lies in state at Birla House.

The funeral pyre at Rajghat, Delhi on January 31. 151

**The urn containing Gandhi's ashes being carried from Birla House
on February 11, 1948.**

The urn being moved through Delhi.

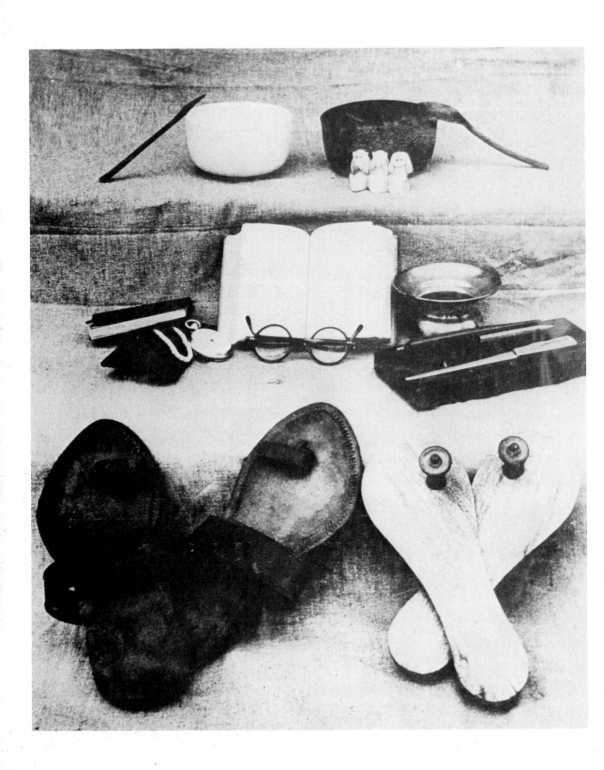

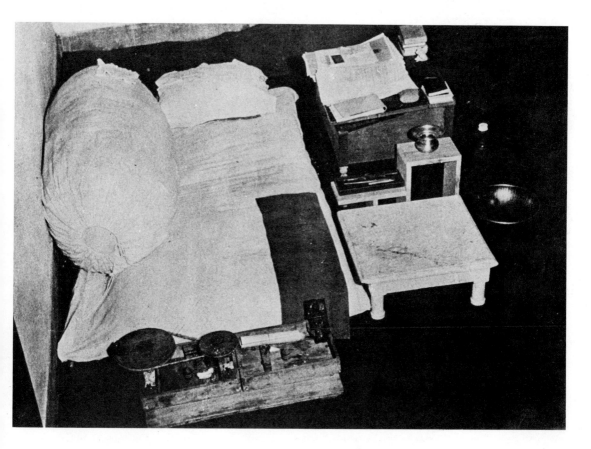

Three photographs of Gandhi's personal possessions and furniture.

Afterword   by Richard Attenborough

To make a film about the life of Mahatma Gandhi is an awesome responsibility. Indians revere him as a holy man who led India to independence after centuries as a British colony. Gandhi showed us all how to achieve political change by means of non-violent—but active—civil protest, and I believe his method of peaceful protest is increasingly relevant in today's troubled world.

In 1962 Motilal Kothari, an Indian civil servant living in London, asked me to make a film about Gandhi. I read a biography and some of the Mahatma's own words before making what eventually became a 20-year commitment to completing the film. When I began to research in India itself, I discovered that the bibliography on Gandhi is more extensive than for almost any other person except Christ. In addition, he was also one of the most photographed people of the 20th century—perhaps even more so than Franklin D. Roosevelt or Winston Churchill.

My main goal in making the film was to be as faithful as possible to the spirit of the man. I wanted to discover the truth about Gandhi by studying all the available material. If, in compressing the 79 years of his life into a motion picture of just over three hours duration, I had to depart from certain historical facts, it was essential

that accurate research made me aware of exactly what cinematic liberties I was taking. If I were to depart from information that was incorrect in the first place, I would be in danger of arriving at totally unacceptable decisions.

A biography is someone's opinion containing conscious or unconscious biases. A photograph is a fact—a frozen moment in time—even when you don't know all the circumstances surrounding its existence. The film I hope presents the visual as well as the philosophical truth about Gandhi, and the former derives largely from a vast number of historical photographs which we studied minutely.

The Gandhi National Museum in New Delhi covers two floors of a building close to Rajghat, the site of the Gandhi Memorial near the Yamuna River where Gandhi's body was cremated in 1948. Officials there were immensely cooperative in showing me their collection of photographs and in printing huge blow-ups for reference purposes. I have since discovered that almost every picture ever taken of Gandhi by people all over the world has been donated to the museum. Ironically, some of the oldest pictures from large glass plate negatives, dating back to the last century, are of better quality than later photographs preserved on film.

tor Ben Kingsley (left) as Gandhi and rector Richard Attenborough.

Gandhi as a young lawyer in South Africa.

Ben Kingsley in the film.

All of these helped us in making *Gandhi*. Some determined the concept, set-up, and composition of sequences in the film. Often we framed a scene in exactly the same position and with the same light source as the original photographer. The archive photographs showed postures, clothing, personal relationships and attitudes that helped the screenwriter, the actors and all of us to bring authenticity to various settings and characterizations.

As an actor myself, I know that lack of confidence can detrimentally inhibit a performance. When an actor walks onto a movie set, he is surrounded by people who wonder whether he will make a fool of himself or whether there will be a truth in what he is doing. Anything that can give him an insight into characterization grants him confidence. The resultant authority helps him to relax so that he can take risks, venture into giving a performance of which he was almost unaware he was capable. Historical photographs gave the actors in *Gandhi* their confidence because they could see exactly what they were aiming for visually.

Ben Kingsley, who gives a brilliant performance as Gandhi has to depict some 54 years of his life. Ben, who is in his late thirties, had to go far beyond what one would assume his normal physical capabilities to be. The fact that he could look at a still and see for himself how Gandhi dressed or

At left, Gandhi.

Ben Kingsley.

held his head or wore his hair gave him great assurance. As director, I could talk to Ben for hours on end and still be unable to help him in the same way as one archive photograph.

All the actors playing historical characters such as Gandhi's wife

Actor Ben Kingsley.

At left, Gandhi.

Gandhi's wife Kasturba in 1915.

Kasturba, Nehru, Patel, Kriplani and Jinnah relied on photographs to help build their characters.

The pictures of Gandhi gathering salt from the Indian Ocean beach at Dandi after his famous 241-mile march provide a good example of how archive material helped to set the mood. Gandhi was a very gentle man. I have never seen a picture of him in an aggressive posture. One so often sees him with a marvelous grin on his face giving a characteristic little wave of his hand. We framed the scene of Ben picking up salt exactly as it was in the photo. He positioned his feet and hands in just the same way that Gandhi did. He even held the salt high above his head—emulating perfectly the one defiant gesture of the

Rohini Hattangady as Kasturba in the film.

A house in the Sabarmati *ashram* when Gandhi lived there.

Mahatma's life—as he claimed it as the birthright of the Indian people.

Every department on the film—props, wardrobe, set construction—used massive files of stills. The makeup for each character had to be carefully worked out before we went into production. Once we started shooting there was no time to improvise. To play Gandhi in his seventies, Ben had to be in the makeup chair at 5:30 a.m. in order to appear on the set by 9:30 a.m.

It was not easy to show characters in different stages of aging over the 54

years covered by the film. At some periods in his life Gandhi shaved his whole head, at others only part of it. Now and then he let his hair grow on the sides. Only the archive pictures demonstrated this clearly and factually. If we had followed an apparently logical process of aging without recourse to them the movie could necessarily have been predictable. But, captured in the photographs, Gandhi might look at a particular time very elderly and frail. Two years later he would seem comparatively young again, just as all of us probably go through such changes in appearance due to ill health, diet and prevailing circumstances.

Gandhi's teeth were important in indicating his age as gradually they fell out or were extracted until finally he wore false ones. He used seven different pairs of glasses, interchanging them at various times. He also had a cheap watch hanging from a piece of cord tied around his waist. All these we copied precisely from the photographs.

Many people remember Gandhi as a little old man dressed in a sheet and carrying a beanpole for a staff. He had four staffs of various shapes and sizes. On the Salt March he carried one different from any he had used on previous occasions. Reporters covering the Salt March never wrote that this was 54 inches long. Only the photographs could give us this detail.

Gandhi had several different spinning wheels, or *charkas*, and he held the thread in a particular way when he spun. We were able to capture these idiosyncrasies while Ben was spinning.

We built from scratch an exact replica of Gandhi's *ashram* at Sabarmati. In reality, it was outside Ahmadabad, but we reconstructed it on the river outside Delhi. Every building, every fence and every cooking pot was recreated from the photographs. We were even lucky enough to have the time to plant and grow crops that were historically accurate.

Photographs even helped with the music for the film. I was at a loss to know how to cope with the beginning of the Salt March until I noticed in a still a marcher carrying a single-stringed Indian instrument.

The *ashram* as built from scratch for the film.

Gandhi picking up salt at Dandi, 1930.

At right, the scene in the film.

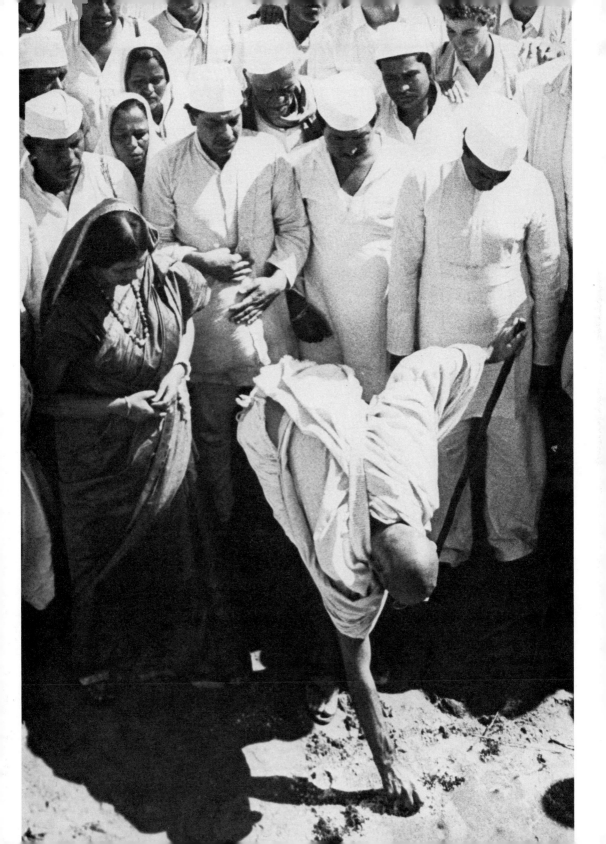

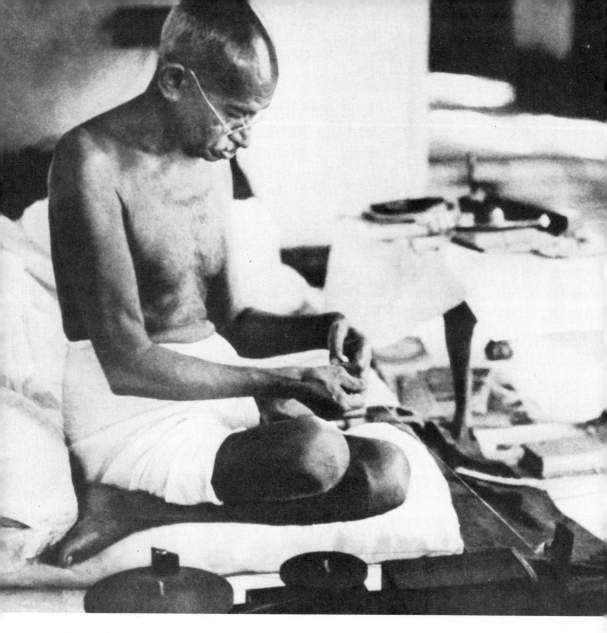

Gandhi at his spinning wheel.

At right, Ben Kingsley.

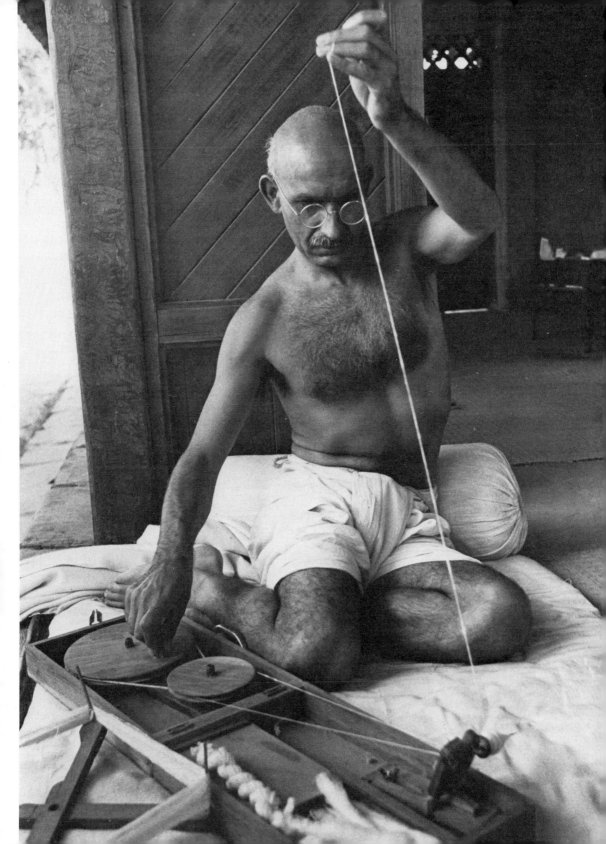

India's first prime minister, Jawaharlal Nehru, was a close associate of Gandhi's over many years. He was immensely kind to me when I visited him in Delhi in 1963 to request his cooperation in the making of the film. He introduced me to his daughter, Indira Gandhi (no relation to the Mahatma), who later became Prime Minister herself. Mrs. Gandhi has been very supportive to the making of the film, even to the extent of loaning some of her father's clothes so that the tailor in Delhi could copy

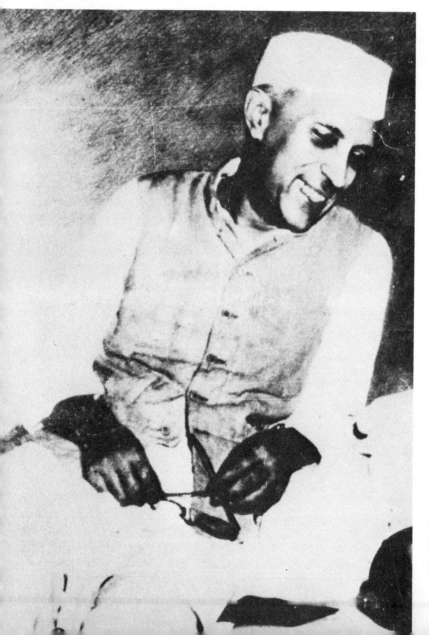

Jawaharlal Nehru. At right, actor Roshan Seth portrays Nehru.

G. K. Gokhale sits third
from right, 1912.
At left, Shreeram Lagoo
as Gokhale.

them for Roshan Seth who plays Pandit Nehru.

We discovered details to help depict all the main characters in the film. Mohammed Ali Jinnah's Saville Row suits, the white streak in his hair, handkerchief in his pocket, ever-present cigarette. The great Indian nationalist Gopal Krishna Gokhale, who was Gandhi's mentor early in his political career—glasses, mustache, tasseled hat, even the way he threw his scarf over his shoulder. Sardar Patel's baldness and the particular shawl he always wore. Lord Louis Mountbatten as he was in his forties when he was the last British viceroy in India—a full head of dark hair, double-breasted suits with wide lapels and two-tone shoes.

Sequences requiring massive groups of people demanded careful attention to historical detail.

· The images of the multitudes who trekked both ways across the Indian-Pakistan border at the time of Partition.
· The Salt March. Which people walked beside Gandhi?
· Cotton mill workers in the north of England. In 1931 Gandhi attended a Round Table Conference in London and characteristically insisted on visiting Yorkshire textile factories which were suffering from the impact of his campaign for India to stop importing British cloth. He explained to the mill-hands that while their circumstances might be difficult, in India the jobless were actually starving.

· Gandhi walking to public prayers in the garden at Birla House in New Delhi during the last days of his life, leaning on his two great-nieces. He was assassinated there on January 30, 1948. The fine *Life* photo-journalist Margaret Bourke-White had been visiting him and taking pictures only two hours beforehand.

Hundreds of thousands of people crowded New Delhi on January 31, 1948, to watch Gandhi's funeral procession. A stunned world followed the event by radio and by newspaper reports and pictures. We assembled a crowd of 200,000 by appealing on radio and television and in newspapers for people to help recreate part of the procession on the 33rd anniversary of Gandhi's death. We also transported 85,000 villagers into Delhi from the countryside, to which were added servicemen and mourners bringing the total of those present to over 300,000. I had never directed a scene involving such a vast mass of humanity, but the photographs showed us precisely where to place the onlookers along the route of the cortege; which people, including Nehru and Patel, actually stood on the bier; who paced behind it; how to position the military personnel and how we should dress the mourners in the procession.

I shall never forget that day. I was humbled by the same sentiment that Albert Einstein had so eloquently voiced: "Generations to come will scarce believe that such a one as this ever in flesh and blood walked upon this earth."

Gandhi with Mohammed Ali Jinnah.

At right, Alyque Padamsee as Jinnah.

Mountbatten, Gandhi and Lady Mountbatten in 1947.

Peter Harlowe as Lord Mountbatten in the film.

Gandhi with English cotton mill workers, 1931.

**Actors portray Gandhi with women workers
at a Lancashire cotton mill.**

**Gandhi supported by his
great-nieces.**

A similar scene in the film.

Gandhi at Birla House, 1948.

A film scene taken at Birla House, Delhi.

The real life funeral procession.

At right, as it was recreated for the mov

Gandhi's India

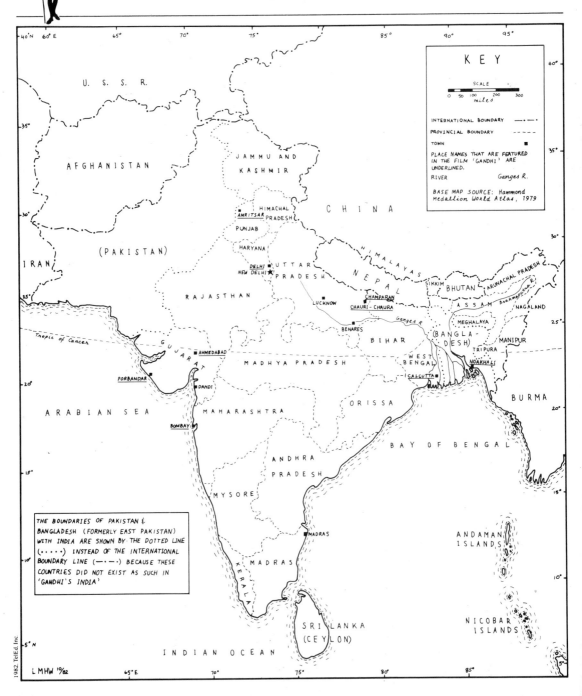

KEY

SCALE

0 50 100   200   300
miles

INTERNATIONAL BOUNDARY —·—·—
PROVINCIAL BOUNDARY — — —
TOWN ■
PLACE NAMES THAT ARE FEATURED IN THE FILM 'GANDHI' ARE UNDERLINED.
RIVER Ganges R.

BASE MAP SOURCE: Hammond Medallion World Atlas, 1979

THE BOUNDARIES OF PAKISTAN & BANGLADESH (FORMERLY EAST PAKISTAN) WITH INDIA ARE SHOWN BY THE DOTTED LINE (·····) INSTEAD OF THE INTERNATIONAL BOUNDARY LINE (—·—·—) BECAUSE THESE COUNTRIES DID NOT EXIST AS SUCH IN 'GANDHI'S INDIA'

1982. TelEd. Inc

L MHW 19/82

Bibliography

Ashe, Geoffrey. *Gandhi*. New York: Stein & Day, 1968.

Attenborough, Richard. *In Search of Gandhi*. London: Bodley Head; Piscataway, N.J.: New Century Publishers, 1983.

Briley, John. *Gandhi* (film script). Richmond Green, Surrey: Indo-British Films Ltd., Oct. 2, 1980.

Coolidge, Olivia. *Gandhi*. Boston: Houghton Mifflin, 1971.

Edwardes, Michael. *Bound to Exile: The Victorians in India*. New York and Washington: Praeger, 1970.

———. *The Last Years of British India*. Cleveland and New York: World, 1963.

Erikson, Erik H. *Gandhi's Truth: On the Origins of Militant Nonviolence*. New York: Norton, 1969.

Fischer, Louis. *Gandhi: His Life and Message for the World*. New York: New American Library, 1954.

———. *The Life of Mahatma Gandhi*. New York: Harper & Row, 1950.

Gandhi, Mohandas Karamchand. *Satyagraha (Nonviolent Resistance)*. Ahmadabad, India: Navajivan Publishing House, 1951.

———. *The Essential Gandhi: His Life, Work and Ideas. An Anthology*. Ed. by Louis Fischer. New York: Vintage Books, 1962.

———. *The Collected Works of Mahatma Gandhi*. Publications Division, Ministry of Information and Broadcasting, Government of India. Selected volumes, Ahmadabad, India: Navajivan Press.

———. *An Autobiography: The Story of My Experiments with Truth*. Boston: Beacon, 1957.

———. *Selected Writings of Mahatma Gandhi*. Selected and introduced by Ronald Duncan. Boston: Beacon, 1951.

———. *The Words of Gandhi*. Selection and introduction by Richard Attenborough. New York: Newmarket Press, 1982.

Green, Martin. *The Challenge of the Mahatmas*. New York: Basic Books, 1978.

Hodson, H. V. *The Great Divide: Britain-India-Pakistan*. New York: Atheneum, 1971.

Jack, Homer A., ed. *The Gandhi Reader: A Source Book of His Life and Writings*. Bloomington: Indiana University Press, 1956.

Kytle, Calvin. *Gandhi, Soldier of Nonviolence: His Effect on India and the World Today*. New York: Grosset & Dunlap, 1969.

Lall, Arthur. *The Emergence of Modern India*. New York: Columbia University Press, 1981.

Mehta, Ved. *Mahatma Gandhi and His Apostles.* New York: Viking, 1977.

Morris, John. *Eating the Indian Air.* New York: Atheneum, 1969.

Naipaul, V. S. *An Area of Darkness.* New York: Vintage Books, 1981 (1964).

————. *India: A Wounded Civilization.* New York: Knopf, 1977.

Nanda, B. R. *Gandhi: A Pictorial Biography.* New Delhi: Ministry of Information and Broadcasting, Publications Division, 1972.

————. *Mahatma Gandhi: A Biography.* New Delhi: Allied Publishers Private Ltd., 1958/1968.

Nehru, Jawaharlal. *Nehru on Gandhi: A Selection, Arranged in the Order of Events, from the Writings and Speeches of Jawaharlal Nehru.* New York: John Day, 1948.

New York Times. Morgue files, esp. Jan. 31, 1948, pp. 1, 3.

Payne, Robert. *The Life and Death of Mahatma Gandhi.* New York: Dutton, 1969.

Shirer, William L. *Gandhi: A Memoir.* New York: Simon & Schuster, 1979.

Shridharani, Krishnalal. *The Mahatma and the World.* New York: Duell, Sloan and Pearce, 1946.

Theroux, Paul. *The Great Railway Bazaar: By Train Through Asia.* Boston: Houghton Mifflin, 1975.

Wolpert, Stanley. *A New History of India.* New York: Oxford University Press, 1977.

Woodcock, George. *Mohandas Gandhi.* Ed. Frank Kermode (Modern Masters series). New York: Viking, 1971.

Index

Page numbers in italics refer to photographs.

190   ART CENTER COLLEGE OF DESIGN LIBRARY
1700 LIDA STREET
PASADENA, CALIFORNIA 91103

About the Authors

GERALD GOLD has been correspondent and editor of *The New York Times* since 1950. Currently story editor with the *Times* Magazine, he has been Deputy Culture Editor, Deputy Foreign Editor, and was chief editor of *The Pentagon Papers, The Watergate Hearings,* and *The White House Transcripts.*

RICHARD ATTENBOROUGH's international fame and stage career as an actor, producer and director spans 40 years. He has acted in *The Great Escape, The Sand Pepples,* and Satyajit Ray's *The Chess Players.* He directed *Oh! What A Lovely War, Young Winston,* and *A Bridge Too Far.* Queen Elizabeth II knighted him in 1976. THE WORDS OF GANDHI and GANDHI: A PICTORIAL BIOGRAPHY, published by Newmarket Press, are two of the three official tie-in books with Sir Richard's film, *Gandhi.* (The third, *In Search of Gandhi,* Attenborough's lavishly illustrated account of the struggle to make the movie, is published by New Century.) All three works result from his 20-year study of biographies, Gandhi's books, articles, speeches, and photographs, and from a family heritage which placed learning, teaching, and concern for human rights at the highest priority. (His brother, David, is the author of *Life on Earth.*)

ART CENTER COLLEGE OF DESIGN LIBRARY
1700 LIDA STREET
PASADENA, CALIFORNIA 91103

28 1 4   6